Happy Tailgating!

Jayne Oakley & Kelli Oakley

Tailgaters' Recipes and Traditions

Kentucky
TALE
GATING
STORIES WITH SAUCE

by

Kelli Oakley & Jayna Oakley

International Standard Book Number 0-9761144-0-2
Library of Congress Card Catalog Number 2004096995

Cover design and book layout by Asher Graphics
Front cover photo by James Asher

Manufactured in the United States of America

All book order correspondence should be addressed to:

Oakley Press
P.O. Box 911031
Lexington, KY 40591-1031
email:oakleys@oakleypress.net
Tel: 1 859 494 1027
Tel: 1 859 433 6495
www.oakleypress.net

Authors' Acknowledgments

From Jayna Oakley:

Thanks, first and foremost, always goes to my family ... my Mom and Dad for always supporting everything I take on and saying "go for it": my brothers, Eddie and Rodney, for not running from anything I ask them to do; my sister-in-law, Beth, for just shaking her head at another one of "our" schemes; my niece and nephews, Ryan, Josh, Alyssa and Nathan, for adding new life to everything I do; my Grannie for her continuous unconditional love and willingness to drop everything to help me; to my best-ever friend Judy for everything she has been, done and said to me for 25-plus years; to Tricia for her wonderful wit and creativity; to Hannah for always believing I could do anything; to Jackie for her friendship and "words-smith" ability; to Todd for getting us started and giving us a name; to Sara for believing she would read a book by me some day; to Jessica for giving me a much-needed push; for all those who participated in this project; and last, to my sister-in-law Kelli, who has become a "sister" I've always wanted and who has wrestled with every business idea and scheme we've thought up! We finally did it! Thanks to everyone!

From Kelli Oakley:

First, a praise to God for giving us the ability and the means to move forward with this project; a great many thanks go out to my family ... especially my dear husband and friend, Eddie, and my two very special sons, Ryan and Josh, all three of whom have been my greatest fans and taste-testers; to my Mom and Dad for their support in whatever the venture might be – and there have been many; to a very special grandmother, "Memmaw," whose footsteps I have strived to follow in when it comes to cooking; to a special "Granny" that reminds me the sky is the limit; to a dear friend, Lish – who has been a true friend and encourager in all times; to my mother-in-law and father-in-law, "Mr. and Mrs. Oak," who have also been taste-testers and great supporters; to the special friends who have encouraged me to keep moving on with my dreams; and finally, Jayna, my friend, sister-in-law, and business partner – she makes every venture an adventure! Thank you to all for the support, love and patience shown throughout this endeavor!

TABLE OF CONTENTS

Hail Marys:
An Introduction to Tailgating

Any football fan who has braved the frigid temperatures and the thermometer-breaking heat waves knows that tailgating is an important part of any football game in Kentucky. From stoking the fires of their grills to keeping ice chests full of their favorite drinks and ales to the camaraderie of reuniting with friends to remember football days and seasons gone by...tailgating has truly become TALEgating to all these Kentucky fanatics!

For just a few Saturdays in the fall, football junkies, reportedly as far back as the 1930's, have been eating, drinking, laughing, talking, singing, dancing, reminiscing about the games that were and predicting the games that will be! It has always been about the game, dressing in their favorite team colors, predicting the outcomes, meeting and talking with opposing school fan talegaters, posing for photos, getting mascots painted on your face, catching up with old friends, waiting in line for the port-a-potties, arguing with friends about the play that turned things around, planning road trips, flying flags to show school spirit, praying, hoping it doesn't rain or snow or get too hot, looking for extra tickets, getting rid of tickets and saying, "I remember when..." and mostly hoping it doesn't have to end in November!

Through this collection of recipes and photos, fans from different schools, of all ages, races, religions and backgrounds have shared their stories of relationships built through bumper to bumper parking lots of smoking grills and stories told by the fireside. Many of the recipes collected for this edition have been passed down from generation to generation of talegaters and football fans.

Kentucky TALEgating: Stories With Sauce will bring to life these tales, photos and favorite foods of Kentucky's die-hard fans and their unpredictable weather, favorite teams and most memorable moments from over 30 years ago.

Playbook:
A Play by Play of Tailgating

Getting ready for an upcoming season of football in Kentucky usually means realizing you have to pack several types of clothing for all of Kentucky's fickle weather. Once you have this gear packed, which may include raincoats, overcoats, extra socks and other apparel in your school colors, you can pretty much leave it in your vehicle for the remainder of the season or until you need to use it. Remember, just like the change of possessions in a game, so is Kentucky's unpredictable weather!

Now, it's time to begin planning your menu. Make sure you do the prep work a day or two before the game. This is where you will want to remember to keep the menu simple so that you'll have time to enjoy old friends and tantalize new neighboring tailgaters. Bring food prepared and stored in disposable containers or bring food you can throw on a grill. For the "social tailgater," you can also stop on the way to the game and buy something ready to eat.

Whether you cook or bring food already prepared, make a list of the items you plan on taking, including paper dinnerware, trash bags and damp towels. No matter how large your party of tailgaters, remember, too, you will be sharing with wanted and unwanted neighbors and new friends, so bring lots of everything!

If you plan on cooking, make sure you've filled your propane tanks or have brought plenty of charcoal, lighter fluid and matches. No fire site is complete without tables and chairs. You will want to arrive at least three or four hours early to begin your whole cooking process, as well as to find a great parking space. If at all possible, park near a grassy spot or at the end of a parking row — and by all means, near a port-a-potty.

Once your food is on the grill, you will want to spend some time getting out your school flags and decorating your site. If you have electricity, you will definitely want to fire up your boom box and play your school fight song as loud as you can or at least until your neighbors begin to complain. As you continue checking your grill, make sure you tune into your local pre-game show and begin making bets with the neighbors on the outcome of the game. If the game is on television, find a good outside location where you will be able to see the television, both in the sunlight and at night. If you have tickets on the 50-yard line, forget the television, radio and your friends and neighbors!

Some of the most important items not to be forgotten on any tailgate day are a cooler full of ice, bottle opener, first-aid kit, toilet paper, sun block, game tickets, parking pass, jumper cables, grill utensils, antacids, more ice, coffee for the next morning, hot sauce, comfortable shoes, friends and more ice!

Enjoy your tailgating season and the stories, great food and fun you will share with one another!

Bill Clark, Carlisle, Kentucky, enjoys being the chef during UK football games. When he's not cooking, he's busy telling all his neighbors stories and jokes.

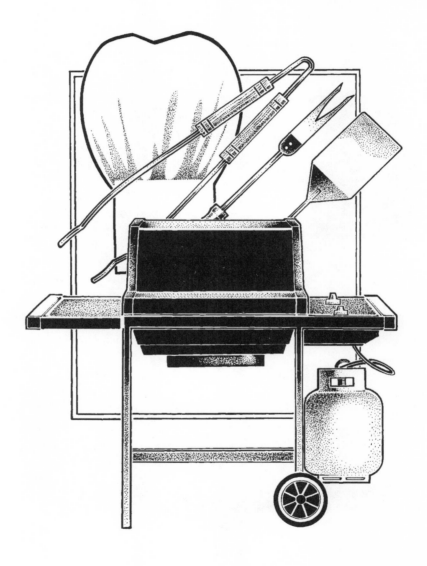

KICKOFFS

Chips, Dips and Other Starters

Caramelized Onions with Barbecue Sauce

2 tablespoons olive oil
2 large onions,
     cut into 1/8-inch thick slices
1/4 teaspoon salt
1/8 teaspoon ground black pepper
1/3 cup canned beef broth
1/2 cup barbecue sauce, your favorite
1 tablespoon apple cider vinegar

Heat the oil in large skillet over medium-high heat. Add the onions, salt and pepper; cook for 8 minutes or until the onions begin to brown, stirring frequently. Add the broth, barbecue sauce and vinegar. Reduce heat to medium; simmer for 15 minutes or until sauce thickens, stirring occasionally. Can be made 1 day ahead. Cover, chill. Heat before serving.

Makes 4 servings.

Shaun Coffey
Russell Springs, Kentucky
Western Kentucky University Hilltopper Fan
University of Kentucky Wildcat Fan

Cheese Ball

Two 8-ounce packages cream cheese, softened
8 1/2-ounce can crushed pineapple, drained
One quarter of a green bell pepper, chopped
2 tablespoons chopped onion
1 teaspoon seasoned salt
1 cup chopped pecans
Pineapple, maraschino cherries and green bell pepper slices for garnish

Combine the cream cheese, pineapple, green pepper, onion and salt; chill. Shape the mixture into a ball when firm. Roll the cheese ball in the chopped pecans. Chill until ready to serve. Garnish with the pineapple, maraschino cherries and green pepper. Serve with your favorite crackers. Can be made ahead and frozen; thaw in the refrigerator before serving.

Don Witt
Lexington, Kentucky
University of Kentucky Wildcat Fan

Cheese Pocket

Two 8-ounce cans crescent rolls
Two 8-ounce packages cream cheese,
    room temperature or
    slightly warmed in the microwave
1 1/4 cups sugar
1 teaspoon vanilla extract
1 stick butter
1 teaspoon cinnamon

Roll out one can of crescent roll dough in the bottom of a 9x13-inch baking dish. Combine the cream cheese, 1 cup of the sugar and vanilla extract in a mixing bowl. Spread the mixture on top of the crescent roll layer. Roll out the remaining crescent roll dough. Place the dough on top of the cream cheese layer. Melt the butter; pour it over the dough. Combine the remaining 1/4 cup sugar and cinnamon; sprinkle on top. Bake at 350 degrees for 30 minutes. Let stand until firm before slicing and serving.

Diane Young
Lexington, Kentucky
University of Kentucky Wildcat Fan

Cheese Spread

8-ounce package cream cheese
1/2 pound Cheddar cheese, grated
1 teaspoon minced garlic
2 teaspoons chili powder
1/4 cup chopped green olives
1/2 cup sour cream
1/2 cup chopped pecans

Combine all of the ingredients; mix well. Spread on crackers. Make tortilla roll-ups by spreading the cheese mixture on flour tortillas; roll up, then cut into 1/2-inch slices.

Jeanne and Ben Carr
Lexington, Kentucky
University of Kentucky Wildcat Fans

Commonwealth Artichoke Squares

1 tablespoon all-purpose flour
8 ounces shredded cheese
3 large eggs, beaten
1/3 cup half-and-half
12 ounces artichokes, well drained,
  cut in small chunks
1/4 cup diced onion, sautéed
1 teaspoon coarse black pepper
1 teaspoon Tabasco sauce

Combine the flour and the shredded cheese. Stir in the eggs and half-and-half. Add the artichoke chunks, sautéed onions, pepper and Tabasco sauce; mix well. Pour the mixture into a lightly coated 1 1/2-quart baking dish. Bake at 325 degrees for about 30 minutes. Cool slightly; cut into squares and serve.

Makes 6 to 8 servings. This is a great dish to serve with brunch food for the early games!

John and Jo Greene
Lexington, Kentucky
University of Kentucky Wildcat Fans

Cucumber Sandwiches

1 to 2 medium cucumbers
16-ounce package Pepperidge Farm
  Rye Cocktail bread
1 stick butter, not margarine, softened
8-ounce jar mayonnaise
Paprika

Wash cucumbers; peel if skin is tough or blemished. Slice into thin to medium slices. Thinly spread bread with butter, then mayonnaise. Place cucumber slices on each slice of bread. Sprinkle with paprika and serve.

Diana Burke
Lexington, Kentucky
University of Kentucky Wildcat Fan
Scott County High School Cardinal Fan

Goal Post Crunch

6 cups mini pretzels, about 9 ounces
6 cups Chex or Crispix cereal
1 cup pecans
1/2 cup butter or margarine
1 cup brown sugar, packed
1/4 cup light corn syrup
1 teaspoon vanilla extract
1/2 teaspoon baking soda

Combine pretzels, cereal and nuts; set aside. In a 2-quart glass bowl, melt the butter in the microwave; add brown sugar and corn syrup and mix. Microwave the brown sugar mixture on high until it boils. Stir once to dissolve sugar and microwave again on medium-low heat for 4 minutes or until the mixture is golden brown. Stir in vanilla extract and baking soda. Pour over pretzel mixture. Toss to coat evenly. Microwave on high, uncovered, 4 to 5 minutes, or until lightly glossed, stirring twice. Spoon onto waxed paper to cool. Break into pieces. Store in airtight container. Can be frozen in resealable plastic bags.

Jeanne and Ben Carr
Lexington, Kentucky
University of Kentucky Wildcat Fans

From the old fairgrounds to new Papa John's Cardinal stadium, 13-year tailgaters from Louisville have braved all kinds of weather to see their team. One of their most memorable moments, despite the bad lightning and fierce rain during a 2002 contest with Florida State University which Louisville won, was the time a friend was tipped over in a port-a-pottie. From left to right are Ron Bailey, Jerry Carr, BJ Morris, Duke Morris and Mary Alice Wilkinson, all of Louisville.

Grandma's Tangy Meatballs

1 pound ground round steak
Salt and pepper to taste
1 egg
1 tablespoon heavy cream
2 to 3 tablespoons all-purpose flour
2 tablespoons butter for browning
1 cup chili sauce
1/2 cup grape jelly

In a mixing bowl, combine meat, salt, pepper, egg and cream. Add just enough flour to hold mixture together. Shape into about 60 small meatballs. In a saucepan with a cover, melt butter. Brown meatballs, turning carefully to avoid piercing. When meatballs are browned, add chili sauce and grape jelly. Cover and simmer at about 190 degrees for 20 minutes. Serve in sauce in a chafing dish with toothpicks handy.

Jennifer Calvert
Lexington, Kentucky
University of Kentucky Wildcat Fan

Ham Rolls

1 medium onion
1/2 pound Swiss cheese
1 pound ham
1/2 pound margarine,
    plus extra to brush on rolls
3 tablespoons poppy seeds
1 teaspoon Worcestershire sauce
3 tablespoons prepared mustard
Four 12-ounce packages
    Pepperidge Farm Party Rolls

Grate onion, cheese and ham in food processor. Combine with remaining ingredients, except for rolls, in a saucepan, cooking until slightly heated. Split open the rolls, spoon the ham mixture on the bottom halves, then replace the top halves. Melt the extra margarine and brush it on tops of rolls. Wrap in foil. Heat 10 to 12 minutes at 400 degrees. The rolls really make a difference in this recipe, so be sure to use Pepperidge Farm Party Rolls.

Coach Judy Cox
Lexington, Kentucky
University of Kentucky Wildcat Fan
Paris High School Lady Hound Fan

Mexican Layered Dip

Two 9-ounce cans bean dip
3 medium-size ripe avocados, diced
2 tablespoons lemon juice
Salt and pepper to taste
1 cup sour cream
1/2 cup mayonnaise
1.25-ounce package taco seasoning
1 green onion, chopped
6-ounce can pitted ripe olives, chopped
3 tomatoes, chopped and drained
Grated Cheddar cheese
Salt and pepper to taste

Layer 1: Spread bean dip in a 1/4-inch-thick layer in a 13x9x2-inch dish.

Layer 2: Arrange avocado pieces on bean dip; sprinkle with lemon juice, salt and pepper.

Layer 3: In a mixing bowl, combine sour cream, mayonnaise and taco seasoning; spread over avocados in a 1/4-inch-thick layer. Sprinkle green onions, olives, tomatoes and cheese on top. Refrigerate before serving. Serve with taco chips.

Carol Pitts Diedrichs
Lexington, Kentucky
University of Kentucky Wildcat Fan

Mexican Roll-Ups

8 ounces cream cheese, softened
8 ounces sour cream, low-fat if desired
10-ounce can mild green chiles, chopped
Green onion, chopped, optional
Garlic salt to taste
1 cup shredded or grated Cheddar cheese
6.6-ounce package 10-inch tortillas

In a mixing bowl, combine all ingredients except tortillas. Spread mixture on individual tortillas. Roll up each tortilla and wrap tightly in plastic wrap. Chill. Before serving, slice tortillas into desired thickness. Can be dipped in salsa or eaten plain.

Wini Humphrey
Lexington, Kentucky
University of Kentucky Wildcat Fan

Morehouse/Gift Family Enchiladas

Ground beef, as much as needed for
    2 enchiladas per person
Cheddar cheese, as much as needed for
    2 enchiladas per person
2 to 3 onions, finely chopped
8-ounce can tomato sauce, as many
    cans as needed to cover enchiladas
8-ounce can tomato paste, as many
    cans as needed to cover enchiladas
Salt and pepper to taste
Tortillas, as many as needed for
    2 per person

Lay out beef, cheese and onion in good-sized separate piles. Put enough sauce and paste in frying pan to get a good covering on the bottom; season to taste. Turn on heat until tomato sauce begins to simmer. Lay out tortillas and flash fry a few seconds on each side until tortilla is firm and crispy. Put down flat on table and put generous portions of cheese, onion and beef; leave beef out for vegetarian. Roll up until everything is firmly in the middle. Place in a baking dish and cover with the remaining tomato sauce and tomato paste. Bake at 325 degrees until cheese inside enchiladas is melted. Cut into bite-size pieces and refrigerate until needed. Can be served hot or cold, depending on weather.

Bob and Jenny Morehouse
Lexington, Kentucky
University of Kentucky Wildcat Fans

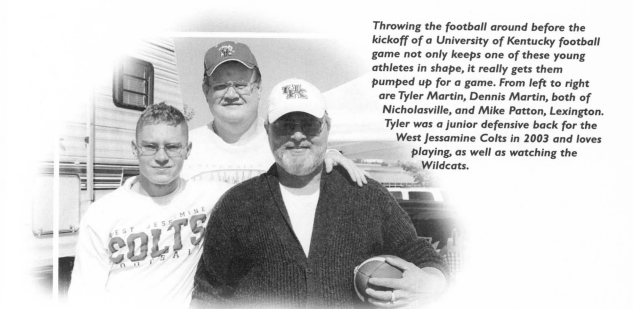

Throwing the football around before the kickoff of a University of Kentucky football game not only keeps one of these young athletes in shape, it really gets them pumped up for a game. From left to right are Tyler Martin, Dennis Martin, both of Nicholasville, and Mike Patton, Lexington. Tyler was a junior defensive back for the West Jessamine Colts in 2003 and loves playing, as well as watching the Wildcats.

Cardinal fan David Hurst, Louisville, sets his sights on the target while tailgating at a 2003 Louisville football game.

Some University of Kentucky fans had some fun roasting a "Cardinal" during the University of Kentucky's August 31, 2003 season opener with the University of Louisville Cardinals. The Cardinals had the last laugh, however, blasting the Wildcats 40-24 at UK's Commonwealth Stadium.

Mrs. Hilen's Chutney Cream Cheese Spread

8 ounces cream cheese, softened
5 ounces Major Grey mango chutney
6 slices bacon, fried crisp
3 to 4 green onions

On a cake plate, spread the cream cheese. Spread the chutney over the cream cheese. Just before serving, crumble the bacon and place it on top of the chutney; chop the green onion into small pieces and sprinkle them on top of the bacon. If made ahead, be sure to refrigerate until time to serve. Serve with crackers.

Sandy Hilen
Lexington, Kentucky
University of Kentucky Wildcat Fan

Nacho Dip

1 pound hot sausage, crumbled
16-ounce jar Cheez Whiz
16-ounce jar salsa, Chi Chi's
   or homemade

In a skillet, cook the sausage; drain. Stir in the Cheez Whiz and salsa. Serve warm with tortilla chips.

Kelli Oakley
Lexington, Kentucky
University of Kentucky Wildcat Fan
Paul Laurence Dunbar High School Bulldog Fan

Sausage-Mushroom Croustades

28 to 32 slices thin bread, cut into
    3-inch round croustades
1/4 pound Italian sausage, crumbled
1/2 pound mushrooms, finely chopped
3 tablespoons finely-chopped shallots
    or onion
1/4 cup butter
2 tablespoons all-purpose flour
1 1/2 tablespoons finely-chopped
    fresh chives
1 tablespoon finely-chopped
    fresh parsley
1/8 teaspoon ground red pepper
1/2 teaspoon salt
1 cup heavy cream
1/2 teaspoon lemon juice
Parmesan cheese

Flatten bread rounds and place in miniature muffin tins. This is somewhat frustrating, but it is worth the effort; they take on various shapes and taste good! Bake at 300 degrees for 10 minutes. In a frying pan, brown the sausage; remove from pan and drain on paper towel. Sauté mushrooms and shallots or onions in butter. Add in the flour, chives, parsley, red pepper and salt; stir and cook 1 minute. Add cream and lemon juice and stir well. Add sausage. Cook until mixture is thick; does not take long. When mixture has cooled, spoon onto croustades and sprinkle tops with Parmesan cheese. Bake at 350 degrees until hot.

Josephine Walker
Lexington, Kentucky
University of Kentucky Wildcat Fan

Spinach Dip

8-ounce can water chestnuts
1 medium onion, chopped fine,
    or 1 envelope Lipton onion cup of
    soup mix
10-ounce package frozen spinach
1 cup mayonnaise
1 cup sour cream
1-ounce package Knorr vegetable
    soup mix

Chop water chestnuts in blender. Drain spinach very dry and chop in blender (uncooked). Combine all ingredients and mix well. Chill for 1 hour before serving. Dip is green in color and is good with raw veggies or chips.

Kelli Oakley
Lexington, Kentucky
University of Kentucky Wildcat Fan

Spinach Artichoke Dip

10-ounce package frozen chopped
    spinach, cooked and drained well
14-ounce can quartered artichokes,
    drained and cut up
6 1/2-ounce Garlic & Herb Alouette
    soft spread cheese
1 cup shredded Parmesan cheese
8 ounces sour cream
1/2 cup mayonnaise
2-ounce jar pimentos, chopped
6 slices bacon, cooked and crumbled,
    optional

Combine all ingredients except bacon in a mixing bowl. Spread in a greased 9x13-inch baking dish. Bake for 30 minutes at 350 degrees. Sprinkle bacon on top after cooking.

Don and Peggi Frazier
Lexington, Kentucky
University of Kentucky Wildcat Fans

Stuffed Banana Peppers

2 1/2-ounce package dried beef,
    chopped fine
8-ounce package cream cheese,
    room temperature
1 teaspoon horseradish
12 to 15 banana peppers, hot or mild

In a mixing bowl, combine first three ingredients. Slice banana peppers in half lengthwise, then fill with dried beef mixture. Can be served chilled or placed on grill for a few minutes to warm.

Jeanne and Ben Carr
Lexington, Kentucky
University of Kentucky Wildcat Fans

Swedish Meatballs

Meatballs:

1 pound ground beef
1 cup bread crumbs
1 cup milk
Salt and pepper to taste
2 tablespoons butter

Sauce:

2 medium onions, chopped
2 tablespoons vinegar
4 tablespoons Worcestershire sauce
4 tablespoons brown sugar
1 cup ketchup

In a mixing bowl, combine all the ingredients for the meatballs except the butter. Roll the mixture into meatballs and brown in butter. To make the sauce, combine all sauce ingredients and cook until onions are tender. Pour over meatballs and serve.

Diana Burke
Lexington, Kentucky
University of Kentucky Wildcat Fan
Scott County High School Cardinal Fan

Swiss Cheese and Ham Rolls

1/4 pound butter, room temperature
2 teaspoons prepared mustard
2 tablespoons poppy seeds
2 teaspoons Worcestershire sauce
1 small onion, grated
20-roll package Pepperidge Farm
   party rolls
1/2 pound thin-sliced deli ham
4- to 5-ounce package sliced
   Swiss cheese

Mix first five ingredients. Split rolls in half. Spread mixture on both sides of the rolls. Layer ham, cheese, then more ham on rolls. Replace top halves of roll and heat in a 350-degree oven until cheese is melted. May be made ahead of time and refrigerated. Can also be frozen after baked.

Wini Humphrey
Lexington, Kentucky
University of Kentucky Wildcat Fan

Tailgating Salsa

Two 10-ounce cans Ro-Tel
   mexican tomatoes and green chilies
14.5-ounce can no-salt-added
   Del-Monte diced tomatoes
1 teaspoon garlic, minced
Salt and pepper to taste

Drain the tomatoes and place all the ingredients in a blender or food processor. Pulse until all ingredients are the same consistency, but not soupy. Chill and serve with chips. If you like your salsa very hot, use the hot Ro-Tel tomatoes and chilies, and for the milder version, you guessed it, use the mild can of Ro-Tel. This salsa is great for mixing with Velveeta and cooked crumbled sausage or ground beef. It can be made days in advance and keeps up to two weeks in the fridge. For larger recipes, simply double, triple, quadruple the ingredients.

My amounts make about 2 cups of salsa.

David Charles
Georgetown, Kentucky
Scott County High School Cardinal Fan
University of Kentucky Wildcat Fan

Wide-Out Watermelon

6 cups cubed, seeded watermelon
1/2 pound sweet cherries, halved
  and pitted
1 cup blueberries
1 cup sliced fresh plums

Fizzy Berry Sauce:

10-ounce package frozen sliced
  strawberries, thawed
2 tablespoons fresh lime juice
1/3 cup chilled club soda

In large serving bowl or giant brandy snifter, toss the watermelon with sweet cherries, blueberries and sliced plums. Cover and chill until serving time, although fruit is always more flavorful served at room temperature. Meanwhile, purée the thawed strawberries with their juices in a blender jar. Cover and whirl with the fresh lime juice. Drizzle fruit in its serving bowl with strawberry purée and splash with club soda.

Makes 10 servings.

Michael Simpson
Lexington, Kentucky
University of Kentucky Wildcat Fan

Zing Wings

2 1/2 pounds chicken wings
6 tablespoons Tabasco sauce
1/4 cup margarine, melted

Split chicken wings at each joint, discarding tips; wash wings and pat dry. Bake on a rack at 400 degrees for 25 minutes, turning over once. Combine Tabasco sauce and melted margarine. Dip chicken into sauce. Serve over chopped lettuce and tomatoes with extra sauce on the side. Great with corn bread.

Jerry Murphy
Lexington, Kentucky
University of Kentucky Wildcat Fan

Buffalo Busters

12 frozen yeast rolls, thawed in
   the refrigerator
2 boneless chicken breasts
3/4 cup Louisiana hot sauce
1/4 cup butter
1/4 teaspoon garlic powder
1/4 teaspoon onion powder
1/4 teaspoon cayenne pepper
Tabasco sauce to taste
2 cups finely-shredded Colby-Jack
   or mozzarella cheese
Bleu cheese dressing

Cut each roll in half with kitchen shears and re-roll into a ball. Place on a cookie sheet lined with waxed paper and coated with nonstick spray. Spray the tops of the rolls; cover with waxed paper and a kitchen towel. Allow to rise in a warm place for about 40 to 45 minutes. Meanwhile, cook chicken in boiling salted water until done; drain and cool. Chop into a fine dice and set aside. Place the hot sauce, butter and dry seasonings in a medium-size microwave-proof bowl and microwave until butter is melted; whisk to combine and add Tabasco to taste; this step can be done in a saucepan on the stove. Add the chicken to the sauce mixture and combine well.

Preheat oven to 400 degrees. Place each dough ball onto a greased baking sheet. Bake for 5 minutes. Remove from oven and make an indention in the middle using a tart tamper, the back of a coffee scoop, or another similar implement. Fill the indentation with a spoonful of the chicken mixture; I use a small cookie scoop. Top with shredded cheese and return to the oven for 7 to 10 minutes or until the filling is hot and the cheese is melted. Cool to room temperature. Pack in plastic ware for transport. Serve with bleu cheese dressing.

Makes 24.

Rebecca L. Flanagan
Lexington, Kentucky
University of Kentucky Wildcat Fan

Fred Wells, left, and Ed Love, both staff members of the University of Kentucky physical plant department, have been working games since the 1980s. They said tailgating has grown every year and they expect it to continue.

UK Employees Start Early on Game Days

Long before tailgaters have begun firing up their grills, the University of Kentucky's physical plant employees are out and about at Commonwealth Stadium putting on the finishing touches before kickoff. Long-timers Fred Wells and Ed Love say they start about 5 a.m. on the day of a noon game and around 9 a.m. for an evening game. Besides making sure everything is up and running smoothly in the stadium, they also double check the President's Room, camera deck, and press box, making sure everything is in place. On cold days, according to Love, it's important to make sure the heat has been turned on and is working. Another task — one not many would think much about, but is a necessity for the Wildcats 70,000-plus fans — is opening up all the porta johns. "We have 85 porta johns that we scatter around the 200 or so acres," said Wells. Ask Wells and Love their favorite part of game day and they quickly tell you it's seeing everyone leave and knowing Kentucky won!

Cardinal Cheese Spread

1 1/2 cups mayonnaise
4-ounce jar diced pimentos, drained
1 tablespoon finely-grated onion
1 teaspoon Worcestershire sauce
8-ounce block extra-sharp
    Cheddar cheese, shredded
8-ounce block sharp Cheddar cheese,
    shredded
1/2 cup pickled jalapeño pepper slices,
    drained and chopped

Combine first 4 ingredients in a large bowl; stir in cheeses. Stir in chopped pepper. Spoon cheese into gift jars. Store in refrigerator.

Nora Bailey
Louisville, Kentucky
University of Louisville Cardinal Fan

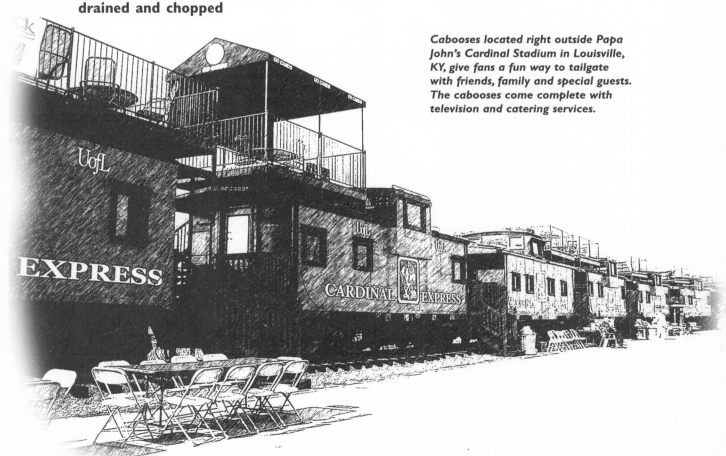

Cabooses located right outside Papa John's Cardinal Stadium in Louisville, KY, give fans a fun way to tailgate with friends, family and special guests. The cabooses come complete with television and catering services.

Country Ham Log

8 ounces cream cheese, softened
1 tablespoon mayonnaise
3/4 cup chutney
1 cup finely-ground country ham
1 cup chopped pecans, optional

Mix all ingredients except pecans, then shape into log on wax paper. Roll in chopped pecans. You may also add pecans to mixture if desired. Freeze/store. Thaw before serving. Serve with crackers.

Bonnie Mays
Lexington, Kentucky
University of Kentucky Wildcat Fan

Black Bean Salsa

Two 16-ounce cans black beans, rinsed
Two 11-ounce cans white
   Shoe Peg corn, drained
Two 4-ounce cans chopped
   green chilies, drained
1 red bell pepper, chopped
1 small can chopped jalapeño chilies
1 small bunch cilantro, minced
2/3 cup apple cider vinegar
1/3 cup vegetable oil
Pepper to taste

Combine beans, corn, green chilies, bell pepper, jalapeños and cilantro in a bowl until blended. Add vinegar and oil to the bean mixture gradually; mix well. Chill, covered, for 2 to 3 hours. Serve with tortilla chips.

Margaret Banks
Stamping Ground, Kentucky
University of Kentucky Wildcat Fan

Tomato Salsa

1 fresh jalapeño pepper, seeded
2 green onions
1 yellow onion, quartered
6 cups canned chopped tomatoes,
   about four 14-ounce cans
1 tablespoon salt
1 1/2 teaspoons cumin
1 tablespoon sugar
Half of one bunch fresh cilantro

Put jalapeño in food processor and dice.
Add green onions and yellow onion and
puree. Add tomatoes, salt, cumin and
sugar; blend. Add fresh cilantro leaves
and stir. Serve with tortilla chips.

Jimmy Banks
Stamping Ground, Kentucky
University of Kentucky Wildcat Fan

Shrimp Dip

8-ounce package cream cheese
1/2 cup mayonnaise
1 cup shrimp, peeled and deveined,
   cut into small pieces
1 small chopped onion
6-ounce jar olives, chopped

Combine all ingredients and chill.
Delicious served with Fritos.

Richard Ford
Lexington, Kentucky
University of Kentucky Wildcat Fan

Beer Cheese Spread

2 cups finely-shredded Cheddar cheese
1/4 cup beer
3 tablespoons tomato paste
2 teaspoons Worcestershire sauce
1/4 teaspoon garlic powder

Let the Cheddar cheese stand at room temperature for 30 minutes. In a mixing bowl, combine cheese, beer, tomato paste, Worcestershire sauce and garlic powder. Beat with mixer until combined. Cover and chill for at least 2 hours. Serve with choice of toasted pita chips, crackers and/or tortilla chips.

Rachel Mefford
Lexington, Kentucky
University of Kentucky Wildcat Fan

Taco-Beef Dip

1 pound ground beef
1 clove garlic, minced
15-ounce can tomato sauce
Half of a 1 1/4-ounce envelope taco
    seasoning mix
Several dashes of hot pepper sauce
2 cups shredded Cheddar cheese
1 tablespoon all-purpose flour
1 cup sour cream
1 small tomato, chopped
1 tablespoon sliced green onion
Tortilla chips

Cook ground beef and garlic until beef is browned. Drain fat. Stir in tomato sauce, taco seasoning mix and hot pepper sauce. Simmer uncovered for 5 minutes. In a mixing bowl, toss cheese with flour. Add cheese to meat mixture, stirring until cheese is melted. Transfer the hot mixture to a fondue or chafing dish, then place over burner. Dollop with sour cream. Sprinkle with chopped tomatoes and sliced green onion. Serve with tortilla chips.

Carol Gabbard
Lexington, Kentucky
University of Kentucky Wildcat Fan

Homemade Pimento Cheese

1 1/2 cups mayonnaise
4-ounce jar diced pimento, drained
1 tablespoon finely-grated onion
1 teaspoon Worcestershire sauce
8-ounce block extra-sharp
    Cheddar cheese, shredded
8-ounce block sharp Cheddar cheese,
    shredded
1/2 cup pickled jalapeño pepper slices,
    drained and chopped

Combine first four ingredients in a large bowl; stir in cheeses. Stir in chopped pepper. Spoon cheese into gift jars. Store in refrigerator.

Carol Gabbard
Lexington, Kentucky
University of Kentucky Wildcat Fan

Candy's Mango Dip

8-ounce package cream cheese
10-ounce bottle mango chutney
2-ounce package real bacon bits
6 to 8 small green onions, chopped
16-ounce box Wheat Thins

Soften the cream cheese and spread it in the bottom of a pie dish. Pour the mango chutney over the cream and spread. Spread some of the bacon bits over the chutney, then sprinkle the chopped green onion and remaining bacon bits on top. Serve with Wheat Thins.

Steve and Cheryl Glenn
Frankfort, Kentucky
University of Kentucky Wildcat Fans

Olive Cheese Spread

8-ounce package cream cheese, softened
1 cup chopped green olives
1/2 cup shredded Cheddar cheese
Onion powder to taste
Crackers, melba toast, rye party bread

Mix first four ingredients. Let sit at room temperature for 30 minutes prior to serving to allow for spreading once it has been refrigerated.

B.J. Morris
Louisville, Kentucky
University of Louisville Cardinal Fan

Cheese Ball

Two 8-ounce packages cream cheese
Two 6-ounce packages dried beef; save
   half of a pack to roll in
1 tablespoon lemon juice
1 to 3 green onions, chopped
1 tablespoon Worcestershire sauce

Mix all ingredients together except for the half a pack of dried beef. Form mixture into a ball and roll in the remainder of the dried beef. Chill for 1 hour and serve with crackers.

Connie Tipton
Lexington, Kentucky
Everyone's Fan

Ham Ball

8 ounces cream cheese
1 medium onion, chopped
6-once package ham or beef, chopped

Mix all ingredients together, then shape into a ball. Chill for 1 hour. Serve with crackers.

Connie Tipton
Lexington, Kentucky
Everyone's Fan

Cardinal Chicken Bites

1 pound boneless, skinless
  chicken breasts
1 tablespoon garlic powder
1 tablespoon onion powder
1 tablespoon pepper
2 teaspoons seasoned salt
1 teaspoon paprika
1 small onion, cut into strips
15 jalapeño peppers, halved and
  seeded
1 pound sliced bacon, halved
  widthwise
8-ounce jar favorite bleu cheese
  dressing

Cut chicken into 2x1 1/2-inch strips.
In a large resealable plastic bag,
combine the garlic
powder, onion
powder, pepper,
seasoned salt and
paprika; add chicken
and shake to coat.
Place a chicken
and onion strip in
each jalapeño half.

Wrap each with a piece of bacon and
secure with toothpicks. Grill, uncovered,
over indirect medium heat for 18 to
20 minutes or until chicken juices run
clear and bacon is crisp, turning once.
Serve with bleu cheese dressing.

David Hurst
Louisville, Kentucky
University of Louisville Cardinal Fan

*Taking a breather from tailgating and games,
David Hurst, Louisville, throws a few burgers on
the grill before a Cardinal 2003 football game.*

Fruit Dip

8-ounce package cream cheese
7-ounce jar marshmallow creme
1 tablespoon orange juice

Mix well and serve with fruit — strawberries, grapes, pineapple, apple slices and cantaloupe.

Betty Rose
Lexington, Kentucky
Everyone's Fan

Sausage-Cheese Balls

1 pound sausage meat, mild or hot
1/4 cup finely-chopped celery
1/4 cup finely-chopped green onion
3 cups baking mix, such as Bisquick
1 1/2 cups shredded Cheddar cheese
1 egg, lightly beaten
1 tablespoon butter or margarine, melted

In a skillet, brown the sausage with celery and onion; drain well. Combine sausage mixture with baking mix, egg, cheese and butter/margarine. Mix well; form into balls about 1 inch in size. Bake in a preheated 350-degree oven on lightly greased or sprayed baking sheets for 20 to 25 minutes, until lightly browned.

Makes about 36 appetizers.

Bryan Houck, Editor
Big Blue Nation
Lexington, Kentucky
University of Kentucky Wildcat Fan

Beer Cheese

16 ounces shredded Cheddar cheese
16 ounces shredded Swiss cheese
1 clove garlic, crushed and minced
1 tablespoon dry mustard
2 teaspoons Worcestershire sauce
1/8 teaspoon cayenne pepper, or
   to taste
8 ounces beer

In a mixing bowl or food processor, combine all ingredients; mix well until smooth. Store in the refrigerator in a covered jar or crock. Serve with crackers.

Makes about 3 cups.

Bryan Houck, Editor
Big Blue Nation
Lexington, Kentucky
University of Kentucky Wildcat Fan

Tailgate Party Mix

1 cup margarine, melted
2 tablespoons garlic salt
1/4 cup Worcestershire sauce
1 cup each Rice Chex, Corn Chex and
   Wheat Chex, or 3 cups of any one
   of the three
1 cup Cheerios
1 cup stick pretzels
1 cup Pepperidge Farm sesame sticks
   and/or 1 cup cheese tidbits
10 ounces cashews
22 ounces mixed nuts
7.5-ounce box Bugles

Mix together margarine, garlic salt and Worcestershire sauce, stirring well. Mix all other ingredients in large roasting pan. Pour Worcestershire mixture over ingredients in pan. Mix well. Bake at 250 degrees for about 1 1/2 hours. Stir at least four times during baking.

Linda Herrington
Lexington, Kentucky
University of Kentucky Wildcat Fan

Crab Party Dip

1/4 cup finely-chopped green onion
3/4 cup finely-chopped celery
8-ounce package cream cheese,
    softened
1/4 cup Litehouse (original)
    bleu cheese dressing
1 tablespoon mayonnaise
1/2 teaspoon pepper
2 pounds imitation crab meat, chopped

In a large bowl, combine all ingredients; mix well. Chill. Serve in a lettuce-lined bowl or on a platter surrounded with crackers.

Kelli Oakley
Lexington, Kentucky
University of Kentucky Wildcat Fan
Paul Laurence Dunbar High School Bulldog Fan

Captain's Corn Dip

11-ounce can Shoe Peg corn, drained
1/2 cup mayonnaise
3/4 cup sour cream
1 small onion
2 cups shredded sharp Cheddar cheese
1/2 cup sliced jalapeño peppers

Mix all ingredients together. Chill for at least 1 hour. Serve with Fritos.

Sandy Hilen
Lexington, Kentucky
University of Kentucky Wildcat Fan

RUFFAGING THE KICKER

Salads — Hot & Cold

Grannie Charles' Chicken Salad

8 chicken breasts, boneless
1/2 cup pecans, optional
1 cup diced celery
1/2 cup green olives
1 cup sweet pickles
2 cups Miracle Whip or mayonnaise
Green grapes, optional

Cook chicken and cut into small pieces. In a mixing bowl, combine pecans, celery, olives and sweet pickles. Mix together with Miracle Whip or mayonnaise. Add grapes. Refrigerate and serve.

Louise "Grannie" Charles
Lexington, Kentucky
University of Kentucky Wildcat Fan
Paul Laurence Dunbar High School Bulldog Fan

Lexingtonian Louise Charles has been a University of Kentucky Wildcat fan over 60 years. During one of last year's tailgate parties at the Hilary J. Boone Center on the University of Kentucky campus, Mrs. Charles won several game prizes with her great aim.

Broccoli Salad

4 cups raw broccoli florets, cut
   in bite-size pieces
1/3 cup chopped purple onion
1/2 cup dark raisins
1 cup salted, shelled sunflower seeds
9 strips bacon, cooked crisp and
   crumbled
1 1/2 cups mayonnaise
2 tablespoons sugar
1 tablespoon white vinegar

In a mixing bowl, combine broccoli, onion, raisins, sunflower seeds and crumbled bacon. In a separate bowl, mix together the mayonnaise, sugar and vinegar; stir into the broccoli mixture.

Serves 6.

Wini Humphrey
Lexington, Kentucky
University of Kentucky Wildcat Fan

Cornerback Coleslaw

3 medium, very ripe tomatoes,
  seeded and coarsely chopped
3 roasted red bell peppers,
  coarsely chopped
1/4 cup red wine vinegar
2/3 cup olive oil
1/2 teaspoon salt
1/4 cup sugar
1 teaspoon hot pepper sauce
2 large garlic cloves
1 large head green cabbage,
  thinly shredded
1 green bell pepper, chopped
1 medium onion, very thinly sliced
5 stalks celery, thinly sliced diagonally

In the bowl of a food processor fitted with steel chopping blade, combine the first 8 ingredients. Process until tomatoes and peppers are coarsely puréed. In a large bowl, combine the cabbage, pepper, onion, and celery in a large bowl. Pour the tomato dressing over the vegetables and toss. Cover and refrigerate for 4 hours before serving. You can add more hot sauce if you like it hotter. Try heaping some of the slaw on your barbecue sandwiches! Best made with really ripe tomatoes.

Jayna Oakley
Lexington, Kentucky
University of Kentucky Wildcat Fan
Paul Laurence Dunbar High School Bulldog Fan

Crunchy Romaine Toss

4 tablespoons margarine
3-ounce package ramen noodles,
  broken into small pieces
  (discard seasoning packet)
1 cup chopped pecans
1 bunch broccoli
1 head romaine lettuce
1 bunch green onions, sliced

Dressing:

1/2 cup red wine vinegar
1 cup vegetable oil
1 tablespoon sugar
Salt and pepper as desired

Melt 4 tablespoons margarine in large skillet. Sauté noodles; when they begin to brown, add chopped pecans and continue to sauté until all are browned. Be careful not to burn! Drain on paper towel. Meanwhile, chop broccoli into small florets and place in a bowl. Tear lettuce into pieces and add to broccoli. Add green onions and toss together. In a separate bowl, whisk the dressing ingredients together. Before serving, add some of the dressing to the salad; toss and top with nuts and noodles. Dressing makes more than needed for salad.

Nancy Stallard
Lexington, Kentucky
University of Kentucky Wildcat Fan

Cucumber and Onion Salad

3 large cucumbers, peeled
3 medium Vidalia onions

Dressing:

1 cup water
3/4 cup vegetable oil
1/3 cup sugar
1/4 cup cider vinegar
1 teaspoon dried tarragon
3/4 teaspoon salt
1/2 teaspoon pepper

Slice the cucumbers and onions 1/4-inch thick. Combine in a large bowl with a tight-fitting lid. To make dressing, in a medium enameled (not metal) pot, combine all the dressing ingredients. Bring to a boil, stirring over medium heat. Boil for 3 minutes. Immediately pour over the cucumbers and onions. Cover and refrigerate. Serve well chilled. This will keep, refrigerated, for up to 2 weeks.

Makes 6 servings.

Marie Dunlap
Lexington, Kentucky
University of Kentucky Wildcat Fan

Hot Chicken Salad

2 1/2 to 3 cups cooked chicken or turkey chunks
8-ounce can sliced water chestnuts
1/8 teaspoon pepper
2 tablespoons lemon juice
1/2 cup chopped celery
4-ounce jar chopped pimentos
1/2 cup slivered almonds
1/4 teaspoon celery salt
1/8 teaspoon Accent, optional
1 cup mayonnaise
1 tablespoon minced onion, optional
3/4 cup grated sharp cheese
1/2 cup French-fried onion rings

Combine all ingredients except cheese and onion rings. Place the mixture in a shallow casserole dish, about 1 1/2 quarts. Bake at 350 degrees for 15 to 20 minutes or until heated thoroughly. Top with cheese and onion rings. Cook about 15 to 20 minutes longer or until cheese melts.

Makes 4 large servings.

Mr. & Mrs. Carl Gorham
Lexington, Kentucky
University of Kentucky Wildcat Fans

Hot Potato Salad

10 new potatoes, cooked and cubed
1 pound bacon, fried crisp
1 cup mayonnaise
1 cup chopped onion
1 pound Velveeta

Combine all ingredients. Bake at 350 degrees for 30 minutes or until hot and bubbly.

The late Sam Mays
Lexington, Kentucky
University of Kentucky Wildcat Fan

Sam, a University of Kentucky Hilary Boone Center chef, passed away in July, 2002. He was such a kind, caring and giving person, the staff named the kitchen "Sam's Place." His untimely death left a tremendous void but his memory lives on in his "whistle while we work" attitude!

Pasta Vegetable Salad

1 1/2 cups uncooked tricolor
  spiral pasta
1/2 cup fresh broccoli florets
1/2 cup cauliflower florets
1/2 cup chopped cucumber
1/2 cup thinly-sliced celery
1/2 cup thinly-sliced carrot
1/3 cup chopped tomato
1/2 cup ranch salad dressing, or
  more to taste

Cook pasta according to package directions; drain and rinse with cold water. Place pasta in a large bowl and add vegetables. Drizzle with salad dressing; toss to coat evenly. Cover and refrigerate for 1 to 2 hours.

Jayna Oakley
Lexington, Kentucky
University of Kentucky Wildcat Fan
Paul Laurence Dunbar High School Bulldog Fan

Tomato Corn Salad

16-ounce package frozen corn kernels
3 medium tomatoes, diced
1/3 cup Italian salad dressing
1/4 cup minced fresh basil
1/2 teaspoon salt

Cook corn until crisp and tender. In a bowl, combine the tomatoes, salad dressing, basil, and salt. Stir in corn. Serve immediately or refrigerate.

Jimmy Banks
Stamping Ground, Kentucky
University of Kentucky Wildcat Fan

Pineapple Cucumber Salad

8-ounce can pineapple chunks
2 medium cucumbers, halved and thinly sliced
1 cup seedless grapes
2 teaspoons snipped chives
2/3 cup mayonnaise
1/3 cup sugar
1 teaspoon prepared mustard
1/4 teaspoon celery seed
1/4 teaspoon prepared horseradish

Drain pineapple, reserving 1 tablespoon juice and discarding the remainder. In a mixing bowl, combine pineapple, cucumbers, grapes and chives. In another bowl, combine the mayonnaise, sugar, mustard, celery seed, horseradish and reserved pineapple juice. Pour over pineapple mixture; gently stir to coat.

Gary Link
Lexington, Kentucky
University of Kentucky Wildcat Fan

Southern Cornbread Salad

9-inch pan cornbread, crumbled
2 cups shredded lettuce
1 cup chopped bell pepper
3 large tomatoes, chopped
Two 16-ounce cans pinto beans,
    drained
Two 16-ounce cans whole kernel corn,
    drained
1 cup sliced green onion
16-ounce bottle ranch dressing
8-ounce package shredded
    Cheddar cheese
10 slices crisp cooked bacon, crumbled

Layer half of each ingredient in a serving dish in the order given. Repeat layers with remaining ingredients.

Tammy Hatton
Lexington, Kentucky
University of Kentucky Wildcat Fan
Paul Laurence Dunbar High School Bulldog Fan

Hilltopper Tater Salad

8 medium potatoes, cooked
1 1/2 cups mayonnaise
1 cup sour cream
1 1/2 teaspoons horseradish
1 teaspoon celery seed
1/2 teaspoon salt
1 cup chopped fresh parsley
2 medium onions, finely minced
Salt to taste

Peel potatoes and cut into 1/8-inch slices. In a bowl, combine mayonnaise, sour cream, horseradish, celery seed and salt; set aside. In another bowl, mix parsley and onions. In a large serving bowl, arrange a layer of potatoes; salt lightly. Cover with a layer of mayonnaise/sour cream mixture, then a layer of the onion mixture. Continue layers ending with parsley and onion. Do not stir. Cover and refrigerate at least 8 hours. Make this the day before and it is especially delicious.

Shaun Coffey
Russell Springs, Kentucky
Western Kentucky University Hilltopper Fan
University of Kentucky Wildcat Fan
Russell County High School Laker Fan

"Bulldog" Potato Salad

10 pounds red new potatoes
8 eggs
1/2 cup diced celery
2 tablespoons onion flakes
8-ounce jar sweet diced pickles
Salt to taste
1/2 cup mayonnaise
1/2 cup prepared mustard

Peel, cube and cook potatoes until tender. Drain and cool potatoes. Hard-boil the eggs; cool and dice. Mix potatoes, eggs, celery, onion flakes, pickles, salt, mayonnaise and mustard. The mixture should be a little soupy. Potato salad will soak up mayonnaise and mustard and will taste better if prepared the day before tailgating.

Coach Eddie Oakley
Lexington, Kentucky
Paul Laurence Dunbar High School Bulldog Fan

"Commodore" Coleslaw

1 head cabbage
1 tablespoon sugar
1/4 cup tarragon vinegar
1 grated carrot, optional
1/2 cup Marzetti slaw dressing
1/2 to 3/4 cup mayonnaise
Salt and pepper

Shred cabbage as fine as possible. Add other ingredients and mix well. Better if refrigerated for several hours.

Coach Joe Pat Covington
Lexington, Kentucky
Tates Creek High School Commodore Fan

Sizzling Beef Salad

12 ounces boneless beef top sirloin
  steak, cut 1-inch thick
Salt
1 tablespoon red chile paste
1/3 cup lime juice
3 tablespoons cooking oil
2 tablespoons bottled hoisin sauce
6 cups shredded romaine
1 medium fresh papaya, seeded,
  peeled and sliced
2 tablespoons chopped
  honey-roasted peanuts

Lightly sprinkle both sides of meat with salt; spread both sides with chile paste. Place in a resealable plastic bag and set in a shallow dish. Let stand at room temperature for about 30 minutes or refrigerate for at least 4 hours, but no longer then 24 hours. Grill steak until desired doneness. For dressing, in a jar, combine lime juice, oil and hoisin sauce. Cover and shake well. Arrange romaine on dinner plates. To serve, arrange thinly sliced steaks on shredded romaine; add papaya slices. Drizzle with dressing and sprinkle with peanuts.

Charlie Marcum
Lexington, Kentucky
University of Kentucky Wildcat Fan
Paul Laurence Dunbar High School Fan

Cherry Salad

20-ounce can light cherry pie filling
14-ounce can fat-free sweetened
  condensed milk
8-ounce can crushed pineapple
  (in its own juice), drained
12-ounce tub frozen fat-free
  whipped topping, thawed

Combine first three ingredients in a large bowl; stir until well blended. Gently fold in the whipped topping.

Serves 12.

Linda Oakley
Lexington, Kentucky
University of Kentucky Wildcat Fan
Paul Laurence Dunbar High School Bulldog Fan

Macaroni Tomato Salad

8-ounce package shell macaroni
2 medium ripe tomatoes
1/2 cup chopped celery
1/2 cup chopped green onion
Salt and pepper
3 tablespoons mayonnaise

Cook the macaroni according to package instructions. In a mixing bowl, combine the pasta and the rest of the ingredients, using mayonnaise last. Chill and serve.

Linda Herrington
Lexington, Kentucky
University of Kentucky Wildcat Fan

Pasta Salad

8-ounce package tortellini
1/2 cup Italian dressing
1 small cucumber
1 large tomato, cut in chunks
1 small bunch green onions, chopped

Prepare tortellini according to package directions. Add remaining ingredients to drained pasta. Refrigerate overnight or until chilled.

Ann Hughes Powell
Lexington, Kentucky
University of Kentucky Wildcat Fan

Dilled Cucumber Salad

2 large cucumbers, unpeeled and
   thinly sliced
1/3 cup thinly-sliced onion
1 tablespoon fresh dill or
   1 teaspoon dried dill weed
1 tablespoon white vinegar
1/2 teaspoon salt
1/8 teaspoon white pepper
1/8 teaspoon sugar
3/4 cup sour cream

Pat cucumber slices dry between paper towels. Combine cucumbers, onion and next five ingredients in a bowl. Toss gently. Fold in sour cream. Cover and chill for 3 hours. May be served on lettuce leaves on individual plates.

Joann Hughes
Lexington, Kentucky
University of Kentucky Wildcat Fan

Corn(erback) Salad

5 cans Shoe Peg corn, drained
1 cucumber, diced
1 tomato, diced
1 green onion, chopped
1 green bell pepper, chopped
1 cup Miracle Whip
1/2 cup sweet and sour dressing

Mix and eat!

Cheri Freeman
Lexington, Kentucky
University of Kentucky Wildcat Fan

Sensational Sideline Salad

Dressing:

1/3 cup rice wine vinegar
2 tablespoons olive oil
1 teaspoon Worcestershire sauce
1/4 cup honey
1/2 teaspoon garlic powder
1/2 teaspoon dill weed
1/2 tablespoon Dijon mustard

Salad:

1 cucumber, peeled and
    cut into chunks
Half of a green bell pepper,
    cut in 1/4-inch strips
Half of a red onion, peeled and
    cut in 1/4-inch strips
20-ounce can pineapple chunks,
    drained
11-ounce can mandarin oranges,
    drained
1/2 cup raisins
1/2 cup shredded coconut

Combine dressing ingredients and chill in refrigerator.

Mix salad ingredients. Gently toss to combine salad and dressing. Store in refrigerator before serving.

Robyn Hayes
Lexington, Kentucky
University of Kentucky Wildcat Fan

Wild Game Part of Bruce's Celebrity Tailgating

Mention wild game to Bill and Janice Bruce of Hopkinsville and it doesn't have a thing to do with the outcome of the football game or the demeanor of any of the tailgaters. The Bruce's have been serving up wild game for several years and marinate enough doves each year to serve 150 of their closest family and friends…friends who have included celebrities such as former Kentucky governors Paul Patton and the late Ned Breathitt. "I have my own recipe," said Bill Bruce, "that includes a three-day marinade of Italian dressing, green peppers and jalapenos. Once it's marinated, they're wrapped in bacon and cooked for 20 to 25 minutes." Because the dove hunting season begins September 1, Bill said he dresses enough of the birds for football season. On cold, winter nights, he fixes an elk sausage that is just as popular. Janice said her husband Bill was being a little modest about his menus as he is just as famous for his barbecue. "Well, I won't give you my barbecue recipe," said Bill, "but I will tell you the secret to my barbecue is sealing it in your cooler with duct tape. You can leave it in this sealed cooler for up to 12 hours." It's not unusual for the Bruces to feed over 100 people each game either. "We've gone through 200 chickens, five gallons of lemonade and 519 Jell-O slammers," said Janice. The Bruces have been tailgating for several years in the same spot at Commonwealth Stadium with their homemade, oversized, crowd pleasing favorite blue and white grill. "Our sons have been students at UK and this spot is a meeting place for them, their fraternities and families. It's just a great time of year for these great reunions."

Serving celebrities, family and friends through the years from the "Cat Wagon," the Bruce's, of Hopkinsville, have become well-known for their barbecue, marinated doves and Jell-O shots they grill up for the University of Kentucky football games. The Bruces include Janice, Cary, Johnny and Bill.

Asparagus Salad

15-ounce can asparagus spears
8 ounces Italian salad dressing
2-ounce jar pimento

Drain the asparagus, then marinate the spears in the dressing. Serve drained asparagus with strips of pimento across spears.

Debbie Baker
Danville, Kentucky
University of Kentucky Wildcat Fan
Boyle County High School Rebel Fan

Bean Salad

15.5-ounce can kidney beans
14.5-ounce can wax beans
14.5-ounce can French-style
　　green beans
2 medium onions, chopped
2-ounce jar pimentos
1/2 cup oil
1/2 cup vinegar
1/2 teaspoon salt
1/2 teaspoon pepper
1 cup green peppers

Wash all beans. Combine all ingredients; toss and serve.

Sean Marcum
Louisville, Kentucky
University of Florida Gator Fan

Spaghetti Salad

1 pound thin spaghetti noodles
12 to 16 ounces Italian dressing
1 medium or large bell green pepper,
    chopped in small pieces
Small head of broccoli,
    chopped in small pieces
1 large tomato,
    chopped in small pieces
1/2 to 3/4 jar Salad Supreme
    seasoning mix

Cook noodles until medium-soft. Drain and rinse. In a large bowl, mix noodles, green pepper, broccoli and tomatoes. Add Italian dressing to taste; add Salad Supreme seasoning mix. Toss well. Cover and chill overnight or for 3 to 4 hours.

Kim Novicki
Louisville, Kentucky
University of Kentucky Wildcat Fan

Mayor Isaac's Farmer's Market Special

Go to Farmer's Market, West Vine Street, Lexington, Kentucky at 8 a.m. on Saturday mornings.

Buy:
2 red peppers
2 squash
2 onions

Visit with friends. Go home and chop vegetables. Toss lightly in olive oil and put in microwave for 9 minutes. Excellent and so healthy!

Teresa Isaac, Mayor
Lexington, Kentucky
University of Kentucky Wildcat Fan

BOWL GAMES

Soups, Chilis & Stews

Poor Man's Chili

Two 28-ounce cans diced tomatoes
4 tablespoons ketchup
1 large bell pepper, chopped
1 large yellow onion, chopped
2 pounds ground beef
3 tablespoons minced garlic
4 tablespoons chili powder
2 tablespoons cumin
1 teaspoon dried oregano
1 teaspoon salt
1 teaspoon pepper
Three 14-ounce cans Bush's chili beans
Pinch of cayenne pepper or to taste

Pour tomatoes and ketchup into a pot over medium heat. In a separate pot, sauté peppers and onions until soft, then add to pot with tomatoes. Sauté meat with 1 teaspoon of the garlic; drain and add to pot with tomatoes and peppers. Add chili powder, cumin, remaining garlic, oregano, salt and pepper. Simmer for 1 hour. Add beans and simmer an additional half hour. Add cayenne pepper.

Walter Marcum
Lancaster, Kentucky
University of Kentucky Wildcat Fan
Paul Laurence Dunbar Bulldog Fan

'Gator Chili

4 tablespoons vegetable oil
2 large onions, chopped
3 bell peppers, chopped
1 pound lean ground beef
2 tablespoons chili powder
Crushed red pepper to taste
Cayenne pepper to taste
1 tablespoon salt
1/2 teaspoon black pepper
16-ounce can tomatoes
Two 16-ounce cans kidney beans

Combine the vegetable oil, onions and bell peppers in a deep pot. Cook slowly for 20 minutes with cover on. Brown ground beef in a skillet and drain. Add browned ground beef to onions and bell peppers along with the rest of the ingredients and cook slowly for 1 hour. Chili is spicy and hot. Adjust seasoning if a milder chili is desired.

Sean Marcum
Louisville, Kentucky
University of Florida 'Gator Fan

Chili Con Carne

2 pounds ground beef or ground sirloin
2 medium onions, diced
1 medium green bell pepper, diced
2 garlic cloves, minced
28-ounce can tomatoes
6-ounce can tomato paste
1/4 cup chili powder
1 tablespoon sugar
1 1/2 teaspoons salt
1 teaspoon dried oregano leaves
Two 15-ounce cans red kidney beans

In Dutch oven or large saucepan, cook beef, onions, green pepper and garlic until all pan juices are gone and beef is well browned. Stir in tomatoes with liquid, tomato paste, chili powder, sugar, salt and oregano leaves. Over high heat bring to a boil stirring constantly. I use crushed tomatoes. Reduce heat to low; cover and simmer 45 minutes, add kidney beans. This is an excellent thick chili.

Mary Jo Manley
Lexington, Kentucky
University of Kentucky Wildcat Fan
Paul Laurence Dunbar High School Bulldog Fan

Jane and Lou's Very Hot Chili

2 pounds ground chuck
33 ounces tomato juice or V-8 juice
1 medium onion, diced
5 heaping tablespoons chili powder
Hot sauce to taste
15 ounces hot chili beans
15-ounce can diced mushrooms
16-ounce box angel hair pasta
Crushed red pepper to taste
Salt and pepper to taste
12 ounces tomato paste

Brown ground chuck. Add juices, onion, chili powder, hot sauce, mushrooms, all peppers, and salt to taste. Add tomato paste for thickening. Pasta is optional.

Jane and Lou Adams
Lexington, Kentucky
University of Kentucky Wildcat Fan

Kentucky Burgoo

Legend has it that burgoo can be kept going for months and any kind of meat from squirrel, rabbit, venison and bear can be used. I hope you will give it a try. If you are ever tailgating during horse racing time in Kentucky you can give it a try at Keeneland. It is on their menu.

2 pounds pork shank
2 pounds veal shank
2 pounds beef shank
2 pounds breast of lamb
4-pound chicken, such as a baking hen
8 quarts water
2 pounds potatoes
2 pounds onions
4 large carrots
2 green bell peppers
2 cups chopped cabbage
1 1/4 quarts tomato puree
2 cups whole corn, or fresh
3 red pepper pods
2 cups diced okra
2 cups lima beans
1 cup diced celery
Salt and cayenne to taste
Tabasco sauce to taste
A-1 steak sauce to taste
Worcestershire sauce to taste

Put all the meat in cold water and bring to a rapid boil. Simmer until it is tender enough to fall off the bones. Remove from stock and dice meat; discard the bones. Peel potatoes and onions; dice and add to the stock along with the diced meat. Dice remaining ingredients except seasonings, which should be added a little at a time during cooking until it is almost completed. Stir frequently with a long-handled paddle or spoon. Cook until burgoo is thick. Cooking time will vary but the longer it is simmered, the better it is. Recipe should feed about 25 people.

Big John Jelley
Lexington, Kentucky
Official Pig Cooker and Chief Chef of the
Best Big Blue Fans

Cardinal Surprise

1 pound bulk pork sausage
1 pound ground beef
1 envelope taco seasoning
4 cups water
Two 16-ounce cans kidney beans,
    rinsed and drained
Two 15-ounce cans pinto beans,
    rinsed and drained
Two 15-ounce cans garbanzo beans,
    rinsed and drained
Two 14 1/2-ounce cans
    stewed tomatoes
Two 14 1/2 -ounce cans
    Mexican diced tomatoes, undrained
16-ounce jar medium salsa
Sour cream
Shredded Cheddar cheese
Sliced ripe olives, optional

Cook sausage and beef over medium heat until no longer pink; drain. Add taco seasoning and mix well. Stir in the water, beans, tomatoes and salsa. Bring to a boil. Reduce heat and simmer, uncovered, stirring occasionally, for 30 minutes or until heated through. Garnish with sour cream, cheese and black olives if desired. Keep warm on grill.

Melinda Hurst
Louisville, Kentucky
University of Louisville Cardinals Fan

Melinda Hurst takes aim at a "Holy Board" game during a University of Louisville game last year. Also competing is her husband, David, who also serves as chef of the crew. Both are from Louisville. They say the coldest game they ever attended was when the Cardinals played in the Liberty Bowl, and the furthest they traveled was Texas. The two enjoy tailgating with friends Toni and Charlotte Perri and traveling with the Sunny Side Cardinal Club.

Taco Soup

1 1/2 pounds ground beef
1 large onion, chopped
1-ounce package original
    Hidden Valley Ranch dressing mix
1.25-ounce package dry taco mix
Two 15.5-ounce cans hominy or corn,
    or both, with juices
15-ounce can Ro-Tel tomatoes,
    with juices
15-ounce can stewed tomatoes,
    with juices
Two 14 1/2-ounce cans
    ranch style beans
15-ounce can kidney beans

Brown meat and onion. Add dressing
mix, taco mix, hominy and/or corn, tomatoes, stewed tomatoes, ranch style beans
and kidney beans. If you prefer soupier
soup, add water or tomato juice. If you
prefer spicier soup, add another can of
tomatoes.

Betty Browning
Lancaster, Kentucky
University of Kentucky Wildcat Fan

Jim's Football Jambalaya

1 1/2 to 2 pounds chicken, cooked,
    boned and chopped
Salt and pepper to taste
1 1/2 pounds hot smoked sausage
1 large onion, chopped
4 cloves garlic, minced
1 bell pepper, chopped
3 celery ribs, finely chopped
12-ounce can tomato paste
6-ounce can tomato paste
8-ounce can tomato sauce
28-ounce can chopped tomatoes
4 cups chicken stock
2 tablespoons "Tiger Sauce"
1 tablespoon Pickapeppa Sauce
1 teaspoon Tabasco sauce
1 teaspoon cayenne pepper
1 teaspoon black pepper
1 teaspoon white pepper
1 teaspoon dried oregano
1 teaspoon dried thyme
2 whole bay leaves
1 pound smoked ham, diced
1 pound medium to large shrimp,
    shelled
1 pound salad shrimp
4 cups long grain rice, uncooked

Season the chicken meat with a little
salt and pepper; set aside. Brown the
sliced smoked sausage; pour off the fat

and set aside. Sauté the onions, garlic, bell pepper, and celery until the onions turn translucent. Mix the tomato paste with the tomato sauce and brown until it just starts to caramelize. Add the caramelized tomato paste and the chopped tomatoes to the sautéed vegetables, stirring well. Deglaze the tomato paste pan with a little of the chicken stock to the mixture; it should be fairly thick. Add the seasonings and salt to taste. Let this mixture cook for about 30 minutes at medium heat (stir to keep from burning). Add the meat (chicken, ham, and sausage) and cook for another 45 to 60 minutes at low to medium temperature. Add the shrimp 10 minutes before removing from the heat. Make sure the shrimp is cooked. Prepare the 4 cups of rice according to its directions. This should make 8 cups after cooking. Mix the rice with the rest of the ingredients; stirring well. Put the whole mess into a large baking dish and bake uncovered at 350 degrees for approximately an hour. It is best to bake on upper shelf of the oven to keep bottom from burning. This can be frozen for a brief period.

Helen Hague
Lexington, Kentucky
University of Kentucky Wildcat Fan
Henry Clay High School Blue Devil's Fan

When they're not tailgating at the University of Kentucky, Jim and Helen Hague are usually crappie fishing. Enjoying the afternoon weather with friends, seated, left to right, are Marilyn Lockhart, Helen Hague, standing, left to right, Jimmie Lockhart, Jim Hague and Bobby Smith.

Jambalaya

2 tablespoons vegetable oil
1/2 pound andouille or hot smoked
    sausage, cut into 1/2-inch slices
1/2 cup sliced celery
1 small onion, chopped
1 small green or red bell pepper,
    chopped
1 clove garlic, minced
1 1/4 cups chicken broth
8-ounce can diced tomatoes
1 bay leaf
1/4 teaspoon Tabasco or
    similar pepper sauce, or to taste
1/4 teaspoon dried oregano
1/4 teaspoon dried thyme
1/8 teaspoon ground allspice
3/4 cup uncooked rice, such as
    Uncle Ben's Converted
1/2 pound shrimp, peeled, deveined
    and cut in half lengthwise
1/2 pound chicken breasts, boned,
    skin removed, cut into 1-inch cubes

In a large, heavy saucepan or Dutch oven, heat oil over medium-high heat. Add sausage, celery, onion, bell pepper and garlic. Cook 5 minutes or until vegetables are tender, stirring frequently. Stir in broth, tomatoes, chicken, bay leaf, Tabasco and spices. Bring to a boil. Reduce heat and simmer, uncovered, 10 minutes, stirring occasionally. Stir in rice. Cover; simmer 15 minutes. Add shrimp; cover and simmer 5 minutes or until rice is tender and shrimp turn pink. Let stand, covered, 10 minutes. Remove bay leaf before serving.

Bryan Houck, Editor
Big Blue Nation
Lexington, Kentucky
University of Kentucky Fan

Hearty Potato Soup

1/2 cup chopped onion
1/2 cup chopped carrot
1/2 cup chopped celery
15 ounces potatoes, chopped and
    boiled, or leftover mashed potatoes
2 cups skim milk, warmed
1 cup frozen peas, thawed
1/2 teaspoon salt
1/4 teaspoon celery seed
1/8 teaspoon dill seed
1/8 teaspoon white pepper
2 to 3 dashes hot sauce,
    such as Tabasco
1/4 teaspoon liquid smoke
1 green onion, chopped, for garnish
1/4 cup chopped red bell pepper,
    for garnish

Spray a nonstick pot with a little non-stick spray and sauté the onion, carrot, and celery until the onion is slightly soft, about 3 to 5 minutes. Drain the potatoes and add to the vegetables. Warm the milk in the microwave for 5 minutes, then stir into the soup. Add the peas and seasonings. Simmer for 20 to 30 minutes. Adjust seasoning to taste, then ladle into bowls. Garnish with chopped green onions and red bell pepper before serving.

Makes 2 servings.

For potato-cheese soup, put 1 1/2 ounces fat-free Cheddar cheese in the bottom of each bowl before serving.

Jayna Oakley
Lexington, Kentucky
University of Kentucky Wildcat Fan
Paul Laurence Dunbar High School Bulldog Fan

Black Bean Soup

Two 15.5-ounce cans black beans,
   drained and washed
14.5-ounce can Mexican chopped
   tomatoes
14.5-ounce can chopped tomatoes
10-ounce can chopped green chilies
15.25-ounce can white or yellow corn,
   drained
1 tablespoon cumin
1 tablespoon chili powder or to taste
1 teaspoon minced garlic
1/2 cup chopped onion
1/2 cup chopped green bell pepper,
   optional
16-ounce can chili hot beans,
   optional

Put all the ingredients in a slow cooker
and cook on high for 2 to 3 hours. It is
like a chili with no meat – wonderful in
the cooler days of tailgating, and very
good!

Marilyn and Pete Owens
Lexington, Kentucky
Kentucky Roadcats President
University of Kentucky Wildcat Fan

*President of the Kentucky Roadcats RV Club, Pete
Owens, left, chats with Roadcat member George
Eads during a 2003 University of Kentucky football
contest. Both are from Lexington.*

Kentucky Roadcats RV Club Roll Into Stadiums

They start rolling in on Friday evenings for a Saturday game at the University of Kentucky's Commonwealth Stadium. By the time they have all arrived, you can count them...all 95 RVs of the Kentucky Roadcats Club. "This has been so much better for us all to get together," said Pete Owens, founder and president of the club. "We started this club four years ago because we had so many RVs involved and we were never all together in a lot. Now, we have one voice who gets everybody in the same spots together." Friday night tailgaters enjoy a pot luck and an evening of catching up between games. On game day, a 10 a.m. meeting is scheduled to review directions for away games, parking tickets and fundraising projects." We raise money through donations and raffles," said Owens, "and award a scholastic achievement grant each year to a student who is involved with the athletic program but not on scholarship. We gave a $500 grant our first year. This year, we're proud to say that number is up to $2,500." While the Roadcats seem to be the logical answer to any RVer wanting to tailgate, this club has become so much more than that. "We will find any excuse to tailgate," said Owens. "During the off-season, we tailgate at the Horse Park. We have a large alumni following but we're basically just good old Kentucky fans." Owens, who said having one voice for the group has made the biggest difference in organizing for game day, added that the camaraderie shared is the most important part of tailgating ."We have really become one big family," said Owen. "I can't imagine doing anything else on a Saturday afternoon."

Among the 90-plus RVs with the Kentucky Road Cats, vendors set up to sell some University of Kentucky gifts and specialty items.

Over 95 RVs belong to the Kentucky Road Cats RV Club. The University of Kentucky fans travel to several away games and tailgate at the Kentucky Horse Park even during the off-season just to stay in touch.

Clam Chowder

Two 10.75-ounce cans Campbell's
  potato soup
Two 6.5-ounce cans chopped clams
1 cup half-and-half
Medium onion, diced fine
2 cloves garlic, diced fine

Drain one can of clams and save juice from remaining can. Combine all ingredients in a medium saucepan and bring to a boil over medium heat, stirring constantly, for 10 to 15 minutes. Reduce heat to low and simmer for approximately 10 minutes more.

Kelli Oakley
Lexington, Kentucky
University of Kentucky Wildcat Fan
Paul Laurence Dunbar High School Bulldog Fan

Corn Chowder

2 medium potatoes
1 medium onion
29-ounce can creamed corn
11-ounce can niblet corn
Butter
2 cups half-and-half
Salt and pepper to taste

In a saucepan, cook the potatoes and onion in boiling water. Once cooked, do not drain cooking liquid; add cans of corn and continue heating until warm. Put a pat of butter in each bowl and ladle in the hot soup. Add milk, salt and pepper to taste.

Caroline Preston
Catlettsburg, Kentucky
Lawrence County High School Bulldog Fan

Hearty Bean and Vegetable Soup

1 pound assorted dry beans, three or
   four kinds, such as black, red kidney,
   pinto, baby lima, lentil, and green
   and/or yellow split peas
2 cups vegetable juice
1/2 cup dry white wine
1/3 cup soy sauce
1/3 cup apple or pineapple juice
Vegetable stock or water
1/2 cup diced celery
1/2 cup diced parsnips
1/2 cup diced carrots
1/2 cup diced mushrooms
1 onion, diced
1 teaspoon dried basil
1 teaspoon dried parsley
1 bay leaf
3 cloves garlic, minced
1 teaspoon ground black pepper
1 cup rice or pasta, cooked

Sort and rinse beans, then soak overnight in water. Drain beans and place in slow cooker. Add vegetable juice, wine, soy sauce, and apple or pineapple juice. Cover with vegetable stock or water; the amount added depends on whether you prefer a soup (more liquid) or a stew (less). The juice adds just a tad of sweetness and the soy sauce adds depth and the tang of salt. Cook at high for 2 hours. Add vegetables, herbs, and spices, and cook for 5 to 6 hours at low until carrots and parsnips are tender. When tender, add rice or pasta and cook for 1 additional hour.

Jorene Brown
London, Kentucky
University of Kentucky Wildcat Fan
North Laurel County High School Jaguar Fan

Baked Potato Soup

4 large potatoes
2/3 cup butter
2/3 cup all-purpose flour
1 1/2 quarts milk
Salt and pepper
4 green onions
1 cup sour cream
2 cups crisp-cooked, crumbled bacon
5 ounces grated Cheddar cheese

Heat oven to 350 degrees and bake the potatoes until fork-tender. Melt butter in a medium saucepan. Slowly blend in flour with a wire whisk until thoroughly blended. Gradually add milk to the butter-flour mixture, whisking constantly. Whisk in salt and pepper and simmer over low heat, stirring constantly. Cut potatoes in half, scoop out the meat and set aside. Chop half the potato peels and discard the remainder. When milk mixture is very hot, whisk in potato. Add green onion and potato peels. Whisk well, add sour cream and crumbled bacon. Heat thoroughly. Add cheese a little at a time until it is all melted in. Serve with crusty French bread and fresh butter. This is a rich, but great potato soup. Mucho Goodo!

Linda Watson
Lexington, Kentucky
University of Kentucky Wildcat Fan
Paul Laurence Dunbar High School Bulldog Fan

Beer and Cheese Soup

1 cup diced onions
1 cup diced celery
1 cup diced carrots
1 cup diced mushrooms
3/4 cup butter
1/2 cup all-purpose flour
1 teaspoon dry mustard
5 cups chicken or vegetable stock
1 bunch broccoli
11 fluid ounces beer; use a can or
    bottle and save a swallow for
    the cook!
6 ounces grated Cheddar cheese
2 tablespoons grated Parmesan cheese
Salt and pepper to taste

Sauté the diced vegetables in butter. Mix flour and mustard into sautéed vegetables. Add the chicken or vegetable stock to mixture and cook for 5 minutes. Break broccoli into small florets; cut stems into bite-sizes pieces. Steam until tender-crisp. Add beer and cheeses to the soup. Simmer 10 to 15 minutes. Check seasonings. To serve, place some broccoli into a soup bowl and ladle the soup over it.

Coach Daniel Brown
London, Kentucky
University of Kentucky Wildcat Fan
Berea College Mountaineer Fan
North Laurel High School Jaguar Fan

Touchdown Taco Soup

15-ounce can Great Northern beans
15.25-ounce can whole kernel corn
15-ounce can kidney beans
14.5-ounce can tomatoes, diced
10-ounce can Ro-Tel tomatoes
1.25-ounce package taco seasoning mix
1-ounce package ranch dressing

Mix, heat and eat!

Sandy Hilen
Lexington, Kentucky
University of Kentucky Wildcat Fan

New Potato Corn Chowder

2 medium onions, cut in small dice
1 bunch celery, cut in small dice
10 tablespoons real butter
1 gallon milk
1 quart heavy cream or half-and-half
16 new potatoes, cut in medium dice
Kosher salt to taste
Pepper to taste
4 bay leaves
2 tablespoons dried parsley
2 teaspoons dried thyme leaves
2 pinches nutmeg
2 tablespoons vegetable base or
   bouillon cubes
   (chicken base preferably)
8 ounces all-purpose flour
16 ounces cut corn, Shoe Peg preferred

Sauté the onion and celery in 2 tablespoons of the butter. Add the milk and heavy cream and allow to simmer. Add the potatoes, seasonings and base. In a separate small skillet, make a roux with the remaining butter and flour by whipping together until thick and cooking over medium heat approximately 2 minutes; set aside. When the potatoes are cooked, add the corn and slowly incorporate the roux into the soup, whisking while adding. Allow to simmer until desired consistency is achieved. Remove the bay leaves before serving.

Chef Jim Olert
Lexington, Kentucky
University of Kentucky Wildcat Fan

Clock-Stopping Chili

2 pounds lean ground beef or sirloin
3 medium onions, cut in small dice
16-ounce can tomatoes, diced
Kosher salt to taste
Pepper to taste
Fresh garlic, or granulated garlic
   to taste
1/4 cup chili powder
3 tablespoons cumin
1 teaspoon dried oregano
White pepper to taste
Cayenne pepper to taste
Jalapeño peppers to taste
8 ounces kidney beans

Cook the ground beef and onions over medium to high heat until beef is completely cooked. Drain the fat and return to heat. Add the tomatoes (juice and all) and 2 cups water. Add the seasonings and allow to simmer to desired consistency, stirring often. Adjust the seasoning if needed to "kick it up." Add the beans and simmer 10 minutes more. Serve garnished with fresh diced onions, shredded Cheddar cheese and sour cream.

Chef Jim Olert
Lexington, Kentucky
University of Kentucky Wildcat Fan

Beef Barley Soup

2 medium onions
1 head celery
4 to 5 medium carrots
3 tablespoons butter
16 ounces dry pearl barley
2 to 3 pounds cooked beef,
   cut in bite-size pieces
2 gallons beef stock
4 bay leaves
Salt to taste
Pepper to taste
1 tablespoon dried oregano
1 tablespoon dried parsley
1 tablespoon dried thyme leaves
4 tablespoons cornstarch

Dice the onions, celery and carrots; sauté in butter. Add the beef stock and seasonings; bring to a simmer. Add the barley and simmer until it starts to soften. Then add the cubed beef and allow to simmer for 20 to 30 minutes. Dissolve cornstarch in 1 cup cool water. Adjust the consistency of the cornstarch while soup is simmering so the barley is semi-suspended.

Chef Jim Olert
Lexington, Kentucky
University of Kentucky Wildcat Fan

Cajun 15-Bean Soup

16-ounce package Cajun 15-bean soup
1 pound Bob Evans hot sausage
1 large onion, chopped
2 cloves garlic, minced
15-ounce can Cajun stewed tomatoes
Juice of 1 lemon

Soak beans from soup package overnight. Place beans in pot with 12 cups water and boil, covered, 60 to 70 minutes. While beans cook, brown sausage, onions and garlic. Add sausage mixture, stewed tomatoes and lemon juice to beans, along with Cajun 15-bean soup seasoning packet, and simmer 30 to 45 minutes.

Makes approximately 3 quarts.

Sylvia Nutter
Lexington, Kentucky
University of Kentucky Wildcat Fan

Chicken Tortilla Soup

2 to 4 chicken breasts
1 to 2 teaspoons chili powder
1 teaspoon cumin
16-ounce jar salsa
Four to six 14-ounce cans
    chicken broth
1 tablespoon cilantro
15-ounce package frozen corn
15.5-ounce can black beans
14.5-ounce can diced tomatoes
8-ounce can tomato sauce
10-ounce bag Fritos
Favorite cheese, grated,
    to sprinkle on top

Cook chicken, cut into chunks and put into a stock pot. Add all the other ingredients to the pot. Cook until soup hot. Serve over Fritos and top with your choice of cheese.

Rita Griffith
Lexington, Kentucky
University of Kentucky Wildcat Fan

Seth's Tailgate Chili

Meat:

1 pound ground beef or turkey
1 diced medium yellow onion, diced
1/2 teaspoon cumin
1 tablespoon minced garlic
1 tablespoon salt
1/2 teaspoon black pepper

Chili:

14.5 ounce can diced tomatoes, then
   fill three times with water
15.5-ounce can kidney beans,
   drained
10 3/4-ounce can tomato puree
9 ounce domestic beer (sample
   remaining 3 ounces to check
   quality!)
1 medium onion, diced
1 teaspoon salt
1 teaspoon cumin
1/2 teaspoon minced garlic
1/8 teaspoon cayenne pepper
1.3-ounce packet
   Lawry's chili seasoning
2 tablespoons jalapeño peppers,
   finely chopped

Brown ground meat with next five ingredients; drain. Add all the chili ingredients and boil for 20 minutes, or 30 minutes if using beer. Continue to simmer over low to medium heat 30 to 45 minutes, based on desired consistency. I recommend topping with white Cheddar cheese and oyster crackers, although any cheese and crackers work. Note: The beer and jalapeño peppers kick it up a notch but you don't have to use them.

Seth Stallard
Lexington, Kentucky
University of Kentucky Wildcat Fan

Spaghetti Sauce

1/2 pound ground beef
1/2 pound hot Italian sausage
1 onion, chopped
1 green bell pepper, chopped
3 garlic cloves, minced
Lawry's seasoned salt
Two 14.5-ounce cans Italian
    stewed tomatoes
Two 26-ounce jars
    Prego garden combination sauce
Italian seasoning
Dried basil
Dried oregano
Garlic powder
1 teaspoon sugar, or less to taste
3 bay leaves, remove before serving
Cooked spaghetti

Brown ground beef, Italian sausage, onions, green pepper and garlic in skillet, stirring constantly until meat is fine and brown. Before meat is done, add Lawry's seasoned salt. Stir well. Set aside. In large cooking pan, add stewed tomatoes. Mash with hands until tomatoes are crushed. Add meat mixture and stir. Add Italian seasoning, basil, oregano, garlic powder – about 10 shakes of each to suit your taste; add the sugar and bay leaves. Add the Prego sauce. Stir all ingredients together. Cook on low heat about 1 hour, stirring occasionally. Pour over cooked spaghetti and enjoy!

Sylvia Nutter
Lexington, Kentucky
University of Kentucky Wildcat Fan

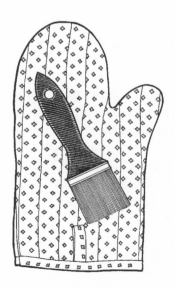

Wildcat Chili

2 pounds lean ground beef
1 medium onion, chopped fine
Half of a green bell pepper, diced
11-ounce can Campbell's
   black bean soup, undiluted
15-ounce can chili beans
Two 14-ounce cans chili-style
   tomatoes, diced
12-ounce bottle beer or ale
Chili seasoning to taste
Dash of cinnamon, optional

In heavy stew pot or Dutch oven lightly coated with olive oil, brown the ground beef until crumbly. Add the chopped onion and green pepper. Cook over medium heat until soft. Add the black bean soup, chili beans and chili-style tomatoes. Mix well and cook 15 to 20 minutes. Pour in the beer, stirring well before adding the seasoning. Cook 20 to 30 minutes at a simmer. Serve with a dollop of sour cream if desired.

Makes 6 to 8 servings.

John and Jo Greene
Lexington, Kentucky
University of Kentucky Wildcat Fan

What It Takes to Feed UK Fans

Marsue Burroughs remembers her company, then Canteen Corporation, now known as the Compass Group, preparing for a University of Kentucky football game day. Back in 1984, she said it was no easy task and took a good seven days to get popcorn popped, sandwiches made, hotdogs and candy delivered, 32 stands cleaned and soft drinks stocked at Kentucky's Commonwealth Stadium. Back then, Commonwealth Stadium seated fewer people than today but, according to Burroughs, who now lives in Charlotte, NC, they had record sales the first game of the 1984 season. That day, Burroughs said, they sold 49,500 22-ounce cups, 6,300 12-ounce cups, 13,200 hot dogs, 1,300 barbecue sandwiches, 975 ham and cheese sandwiches, 3,800 nacho trays, 3,800 boxes of popcorn, 2,850 candy bars, 1,770 sticks of ice cream and 350 packs of 35 cartons of cigarettes. While time has certainly changed how food is prepared and sold, there is still that good old game day food sold today!

No tailgate site at the University of Kentucky would be complete without an inflatable Wildcat.

Reno Deaton Jr. began attending the University of Kentucky and started tailgating. Soon after, his parents would make chili and bring it up to the game for Reno and all his friends. Pictured, left to right, Reno, Jr., Naguanda and Reno Sr., all of Southgate.

From Florida to Alabama to EKU

When Larry Beard packs up to head to Eastern Kentucky University for a Saturday Colonel game in Richmond, Kentucky, he first drives seven hours from his Eustis, Florida home to Elba, Alabama to pick up a day's supply of sausages he grills. Beard, whose son, Jared Beard, was a 2003 senior gridster, missed only one game in the four years Jared played. He would travel about 11 hours, leaving on Friday morning and arriving soon enough at Kidd Stadium to stoke the fires of his grill. Beard says he clocked over 100,000 miles on his truck in three years.

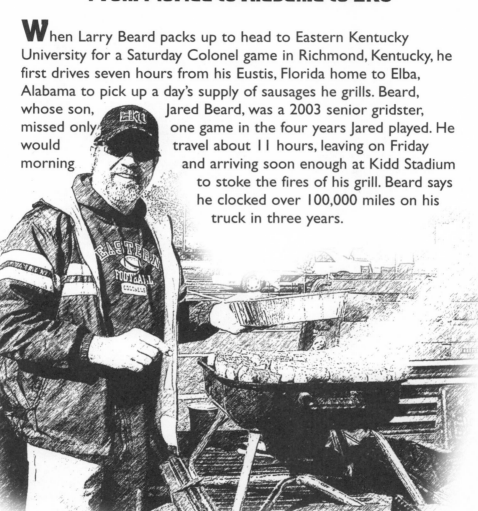

Larry Beard, Eustis, FL, fills the grill with sausages for an EKU Colonel football game during the 2003 season.

BUN WARMERS

Burgers, Hotdogs
&
Sandwiches

Bratwurst in Beer Sauce

8 fresh bratwurst
1 tablespoon all-purpose flour
2 teaspoons vegetable oil
1/2 teaspoon dried marjoram
1/8 teaspoon caraway seed
1 cup dark beer
1 case beer

Place bratwurst in center of grill. Grill approximately 20 minutes, until brats are no longer pink in the middle, turning several times to brown on all sides. In a small saucepan, heat flour and oil over low heat at the edges of the grill. Stir frequently until light brown. Add marjoram and caraway seed. Whisk in dark beer. Bring sauce to a boil; reduce heat and simmer, stirring frequently, until sauce is slightly thickened. Place bratwurst in sauce to coat. Serve with remaining sauce. Makes 8 appetizer or 4 main-course servings. Serve each with a beer!

Gary Link
Lexington, Kentucky
University of Kentucky Wildcat Fan

Corn Dog Cornbread

2 hot dogs, chopped
Two 8.5-ounce boxes
   Jiffy corn bread mix

Roll hot dog pieces into dry mix. Prepare cornbread mix as instructed from box. Bake as instructed from box.

Russ Williams
Lexington, Kentucky
University of Kentucky Wildcat Fan

Crunchy Kraut Dog

1/2 cup mayonnaise
2 tablespoons chili sauce
1 tablespoon minced onion
1 tablespoon minced green bell pepper
1 tablespoon minced dill pickle,
    sweet pickle or drained pickle relish
2 teaspoons minced fresh parsley
3/4 cup sauerkraut
8 wieners
8 hot dog buns,
    preferably bakery-made
3 bacon slices, chopped and fried crisp

Combine the first six ingredients in a small bowl. Cover and refrigerate until needed. Fire up the grill, bringing the temperature to high. In a medium bowl, combine the sauerkraut with the dressing. Grill the wieners for about 3 to 5 minutes over high heat until deeply browned, rolling to crisp all surfaces. Toast the buns on the edge of the grill if you wish. Toss the bacon with the sauerkraut mixture. Place the dogs on the buns and the sauerkraut over the dogs. Serve immediately.

Serves 4 to 8.

Chris Mefford
Lexington, Kentucky
University of Kentucky Wildcat Fan
Paul Laurence Dunbar High School Bulldog Fan

Fullback Burgers

2 1/2 pounds ground sirloin
Half of a large red onion,
    finely chopped
1 egg
4 ounces crumbled bleu cheese
1/2 teaspoon hot sauce,
    preferably Tabasco
Ground black pepper to taste
Garlic salt to taste
Salt, optional

In large bowl, combine beef, onion, egg, bleu cheese, hot sauce, pepper and garlic salt. Gently mix by hand. Gently hand form into 8 burgers. Place in single layer on platter and, if desired, season with salt and pepper. Cook on preheated grill.

Bob Ward
Lexington, Kentucky
University of Kentucky Wildcat Fan

Hail Mary Hot Dogs

16-ounce package hot dogs
1/2 cup chunky salsa
1/2 cup barbecue sauce
8 hot dog buns, split
1 small onion, chopped
1 cup shredded Cheddar cheese

Heat hot dogs as directed on package or grill until thoroughly heated at 160 degrees. Mix salsa and barbecue sauce in small saucepan; cook over medium heat until thoroughly heated, stirring occasionally. Serve hot dogs in buns topped with salsa mixture and onion; sprinkle with cheese.

Ryan Oakley
Lexington, Kentucky
University of Tennessee Volunteer Fan
Paul Laurence Dunbar High School Bulldog Fan

Hot Ham Sandwiches

3 cups cubed ham
1 1/2 cups Velveeta cheese cubes
1 cup chopped green olives
Half of a small onion, chopped
3 hard-boiled eggs, chopped
Mayonnaise
Pickle relish

Mix all ingredients with enough mayonnaise and pickle relish to hold mixture together. Place on hamburger buns. Wrap in aluminum foil. Bake at 400 degrees for 10 minutes.

Linda Oakley
Lexington, Kentucky
University of Kentucky Wildcat Fan
Paul Laurence Dunbar High School Bulldog Fan

Hot Dogs and Sauce

3 pounds ground chuck
1 large onion, chopped
3 tablespoons white vinegar
3 tablespoons brown sugar
4 tablespoons lemon juice
14-ounce bottle ketchup
1/2 tablespoon ground mustard
3 tablespoons Worcestershire sauce
1 1/2 cups water
1/2 cup chopped celery
1/2 cup chopped green bell pepper
Chili powder to taste
Garlic to taste
2 packages hot dogs

Brown ground chuck and onion. Drain fat and mix in remaining ingredients except for hot dogs. Cook for 2 hours. Serve on grilled hot dogs.

Linda Oakley
Lexington, Kentucky
University of Kentucky Wildcat Fan
Paul Laurence Dunbar High School Bulldog Fan

Italian Sausage and Pepper Kabob Sandwiches

1 red bell pepper
1 green bell pepper
1 small yellow onion
Johnsonville Hot Italian sausages, quartered
Marinara sauce
Hot dog buns
Provolone or mozzarella cheese slices

Cut red and green bell peppers in large dice and quarter the onion. Quarter sausage into 1/2-inch pieces. Soak wooden skewers in water about 15 minutes. Take a skewer and alternate peppers, sausage and onions, being sure not to make them longer then the bun you are going to be using. Spread marinara sauce inside your favorite bun or roll. When kabobs are done, place in bun. Hold bun firmly keeping sausage and peppers in place while removing the skewer. Add a slice or two of provolone or mozzarella cheese and serve. Great for a do-it-your-self barbecue!

Walter Marcum
Lancaster, Kentucky
University of Kentucky Wildcat Fan
Paul Laurence Dunbar High School Bulldog Fan

Stromboli

1/4 cup prepared mustard
2 tablespoons chopped fresh basil
    or 2 teaspoons dried basil leaves
1 tablespoon chopped green olives
1 pound frozen bread dough,
    thawed at room temperature
1/4 pound sliced salami
1/4 pound sliced provolone cheese
1/4 pound sliced ham
1/8 pound thinly-sliced pepperoni,
    2-inch diameter
1 egg, beaten
1 teaspoon poppy or sesame seeds

Grease baking sheet. In a small bowl, stir together the mustard, basil and olives; set aside. Roll dough on floured surface to a 16x10-inch rectangle. Arrange salami on dough, overlapping slices, leaving 1-inch border around edges. Spread half of mustard mixture thinly over salami. Arrange provolone and ham over salami. Spread with remaining mustard mixture. Top with pepperoni. Fold one-third of dough toward center from long edge of rectangle. Fold second side toward center enclosing filling. Pinch long side to seal. Pinch ends together and tuck under dough. Place on prepared baking sheet. Cover, let rise in warm place 15 minutes. Preheat oven to 375 degrees. On the top of dough, cut shallow crosswise slits 3 inches apart. Brush stromboli lightly with beaten egg; sprinkle with poppy or sesame seeds. Bake 25 minutes or until browned. Remove to rack; cool slightly. Serve warm.

Makes 12 servings.

Ingrid Judi
Lexington, Kentucky
University of Kentucky Wildcat Fan

Hot Dog Chili

1 large onion, chopped or shredded
2 to 3 tablespoons vegetable oil
10 pounds ground chuck
3-ounce jar chili powder
4 teaspoons black pepper
4 teaspoons salt
15-ounce can tomato purée
6 garlic cloves, ground or
   finely chopped
3 quarts water

Cook onion in pot with vegetable oil. Add ground chuck and cook until meat is browned. Add chili powder, black pepper, salt, tomato puree, garlic, and water. Cook on low heat for approximately 6 to 8 hours, stirring often until mixture is thick and water has cooked away. Note: Must stir well near the end or mixture will stick to bottom of pot and burn. Serve on hot dog buns, with or without hot dogs. Add mustard, onion and hot sauce.

Jimmie and Marilyn Lockhart
Lexington, Kentucky
University of Kentucky Wildcat Fans
Corbin High School Redhounds Fan

Mommy's Fish Cakes

1 can salmon, drained, boned and
   dark skin removed
1/4 cup finely-chopped onions
1/2 sleeve saltine crackers, broken up
1 egg
1/2 cup oil, olive, canola or both,
   for frying

Mix all ingredients well. Make into several thin patties. Fry until golden brown on both sides. Drain on paper towels. Good for sandwiches or to accompany beans and rice.

Lou J. Borders
Louisa, Kentucky
University of Louisville Cardinal Fan
Lawrence County High School Bulldog Fan

Veggie Filled Burgers

2 tablespoons milk
1/2 cup finely-shredded carrot
1/4 cup finely-sliced green onion
1/4 cup soft whole wheat
   bread crumbs
1/4 teaspoon dried Italian seasoning,
   crushed
1/4 teaspoon garlic salt
Dash of pepper
3/4 pound lean ground turkey or
   chicken
1/4 cup Dijon-style mustard
1/2 teaspoon curry powder
4 whole wheat or white hamburger
   buns, split and toasted
Lettuce leaves, optional
Shredded or thinly-sliced zucchini,
   optional
Sliced tomato, optional
Curry mustard, optional

Stir together milk, carrot, green onion, bread crumbs, Italian seasoning, garlic salt and pepper in a medium mixing bowl. Add ground turkey; mix well. Shape the mixture into four 1/2-inch-thick patties. Lightly grease the grill rack. Place patties on the greased grill rack directly over medium-hot coals. Grill, uncovered, turning once, until an instant-read thermometer inserted into the side of a patty registers 165 degrees. Meanwhile, stir together mustard and curry powder. Serve patties on buns topped, if desired, with lettuce leaves, zucchini, sliced tomato and curry-mustard mixture.

Makes 4 servings.

Jessica Smith
Lexington, Kentucky
West Virginia University Mountaineer Fan

Before:
The Bruces Jell-O shot crew posed before they sampled. They include Angela Rex-Barreau, Shane Foley, Brandon Eason, Robert Mackie, Nick Wright, Ryan Smalley, John Emerson, Larry Lehmann and Chad Rankin. Some of the University of Kentucky students are newcomers to tailgating.

After:
Down the hatch with the Jell-O shots are Angela Rex-Barreau, Shane Foley, Brandon Eason, Robert Mackie, Nick Wright, Ryan Smalley, John Emerson, Larry Lehmann and Chad Rankin. The Bruces make over 500 shooters for all the home games.

Pork Patties in Barbecue Sauce

1 cup ketchup
1/2 cup packed brown sugar
1/3 cup granulated sugar
3 tablespoons cooking oil
2 tablespoons white vinegar
1 tablespoon honey
2 teaspoons Worcestershire sauce
1 pound lean ground pork
1 teaspoon sage
8 slices Texas toast, or 4 hamburger
   buns or Kaiser rolls, split
Leaf lettuce
Onion slices

In a medium saucepan, combine ketchup, brown sugar, granulated sugar, cooking oil, vinegar, honey, and Worcestershire sauce. Stir over medium heat until the sugars dissolve and sauce is hot. Cover and refrigerate up to 1 week. To prepare pork patties, combine ground pork and sage in a large mixing bowl. Form mixture into four 3/4-inch-thick patties. Grill, uncovered, until an instant-read thermometer inserted into the center of a patty registers 160 degrees. Turn patties halfway through cooking time and brush with sauce. Serve patties on Texas toast or buns topped with lettuce and onion slices. Pass additional sauce.

Makes 4 servings.

Rodney Oakley
Lexington, Kentucky
University of Kentucky Wildcat Fan

Touchdown Teriyaki Burger

1 1/2 cups soft bread crumbs
1/4 cup chopped onion
1/4 cup water
2 tablespoons sugar
1 tablespoon soy sauce
1 clove garlic, minced
Dash of ground ginger
1 1/2 pounds lean ground beef
6 hamburger buns, split and toasted
Sliced cucumbers, optional
Lettuce leaves, optional

Stir together the soft bread crumbs, onion, water, sugar, soy sauce, garlic and ground ginger in a large mixing bowl. Add the ground beef and mix well. Shape the meat mixture into six 3/4-inch-thick patties. Place patties on the grill rack directly over medium coals. Grill, uncovered, until desired doneness is reached. Serve burgers in buns topped, if desired, with sliced cucumbers and lettuce.

Makes 6 servings.

Karina Karakulova
Lexington, Kentucky
University of Kentucky Wildcat Fan

So Long Sub!

1/3 cup chopped fresh basil leaves
2 tablespoons olive oil
1 tablespoon balsamic vinegar or
    white wine vinegar
8-ounce or half or a 16-ounce loaf
    unsliced French bread
6 ounces thinly-sliced
    mozzarella cheese
4 to 6 ounces thinly-sliced lean
    pastrami
2 plum tomatoes,
    thinly sliced lengthwise
1/8 teaspoon cracked black pepper

In a small bowl, combine basil, oil and vinegar; set aside. Slice bread in half lengthwise. Using a spoon, hollow out bottom half, leaving a 1/2-inch-thick shell. In the shell, layer half the cheese, all the pastrami, and all the tomatoes. Top with basil mixture; sprinkle with pepper. Top with remaining cheese and bread top. Wrap in heavy foil. Transport in an insulated cooler with ice packs. Heat over campfire or on the rack of an uncovered grill over medium heat for 20 to 25 minutes or until heated through, turning every 5 minutes. To serve, cut crosswise into four to six slices.

Makes 4 to 6 main-dish servings.

Charlie Marcum
Lexington, Kentucky
University of Kentucky Wildcat Fan
Paul Laurence Dunbar High School Bulldog Fan

All-American Burgers

2 pounds ground beef
2 teaspoons Dijon mustard
1/4 teaspoon hot sauce
1 garlic clove, minced
1 teaspoon salt
1/2 teaspoon pepper

Sauce:

1/2 cup light mayo-style salad dressing
1/4 cup relish
1/4 cup creamy French dressing
1 teaspoon sugar
1/3 teaspoon pepper

In a mixing bowl, combine ground beef, Dijon mustard, hot sauce, garlic and salt. Form into 10 patties. Grill over hot coals 4 to 6 minutes on each side. Meanwhile, combine the sauce ingredients in a small bowl. Dress burgers with your favorite condiments and spread with the special sauce. Relish the afternoon.

Serves 10.

Deborah I. Back
Lexington, Kentucky
Paul Laurence Dunbar High School Bulldog Fan
University of Kentucky Wildcat Fan

Sideline Sauce for Halftime Hot Dogs

2 pounds ground beef
1 cup water
Garlic powder to taste
Two 8-ounce cans tomato sauce
3 teaspoons chili powder
1 1/2 teaspoons salt
Pepper to taste
1 cup finely-chopped onions

In a skillet, brown ground beef, breaking up any large chunks of meat. Add water, garlic powder, tomato sauce, chili powder, salt and pepper. Simmer 10 to 15 minutes. Makes 5 cups; can be frozen in small butter cups. To serve, heat hot dogs and rolls. Put sauce on hot dogs, then add chopped onions on top.

Nathan Oakley
Lexington, Kentucky
University of Kentucky Wildcat Fan

Chili Cheeseburgers

1 1/2 pounds ground beef
1/4 cup finely-chopped onion
1 teaspoon chili powder
1 teaspoon Worcestershire sauce
3/4 teaspoon salt
1/4 teaspoon garlic salt
1/4 teaspoon pepper
1/4 teaspoon hot pepper sauce
6 ounces Cheddar cheese, sliced
2 tablespoons chopped
    green chili peppers
6 hamburger buns

Preheat barbecue grill. In a large mixing bowl, combine ground beef, finely chopped onion, chili powder, Worcestershire sauce, salt, garlic salt, pepper and hot pepper sauce. Shape the mixture into thin patties, each about 3 1/2 inches in diameter. Divide cheese and chili peppers among half the patties. Top with the remaining patties, sealing the edges firmly. Grill 4 inches from the heat, turning once, until done, about 10 to 15 minutes. Serve on hamburger buns.

Makes 6 servings.

Laura Hayes
Lexington, Kentucky
University of Kentucky Wildcat Fan

Grilled Portobello Burger

6 large portobello mushroom caps
1/2 cup roasted garlic Teriyaki sauce,
    divided
Six 1-ounce slices part-skim
    mozzarella cheese
1/4 cup mayonnaise
6 sourdough buns or rolls, split

Combine mushroom caps and teriyaki sauce in a heavy-duty resealable plastic bag, seal, and turn to coat; let stand 20 minutes. Grill mushrooms, covered with grill lid, over medium-high heat for 2 minutes on each side. Top with cheese and grill 2 minutes more. Spread mayonnaise on cut sides of buns. Grill buns, cut sides down, 1 minute or until toasted. Place mushrooms in buns and serve immediately.

Makes 6 servings.

Sara Bailey
Avon, Indiana
University of Kentucky Wildcat Fan
Paul Laurence Dunbar High School Bulldog Fan

Louisville Knows How to tailgate!

Robin Miller says Louisville is the only athletic office you can call and find out where everyone tailgates! Miller, from Bullitt County, also said the Cardinal fans went through some "tail-grading" several years ago and was honored as the number two tailgate school in the country. For Miller, tailgating is a family affair with her parents and large amounts of white chili on this particular tailgate day. And while tailgating has changed with the move from the old fairgrounds to the new Papa John's Cardinal Stadium, Miller said it's still about the camaraderie. Tailgaters at the new stadium must deal with port-a-potties rather than indoor plumbing and, said Miller, are much more spread out in the new parking lots that in- clude your fans, reserved parking, cabooses, cor-porations and sponsors. Even so, Miller said the Cardinal tailgaters are die-hard fans and will rise to the occa-sion whenever their team takes whatever field.

Martha Lechleiter, left, and Robin Miller say the University of Louisville tailgaters have been rated the #2 tailgate Fans in the nation. Both say tailgating is a family affair and they can't imagine being anywhere else when the Cardinal football team is playing at home.

Lana and Lloyd Petro drove from Deland, FL to Richmond for their son Lance's football games at Eastern Kentucky University. From left to right are Lana, Lloyd and Lance's girlfriend, Katrina Rodriguez.

Double-Decker Burgers

3 pounds lean ground beef
2 large eggs
1/2 cup water
1 teaspoon seasoned salt
2 teaspoons salt
1/8 teaspoon pepper
1/2 teaspoon garlic salt
1/2 cup tomato ketchup
1/4 cup dry bread crumbs
1 onion, sliced
1 tomato, sliced
10 hamburger buns
Prepared mustard for accompaniment
Tomato ketchup for accompaniment

Combine ground beef, eggs, water, seasoned salt, salt, pepper, garlic salt, 1/2 cup ketchup and dry bread crumbs. Form into 20 thin patties. Place thinly sliced onion and thinly sliced tomato between two patties. Press the edges to seal. Grill the patties about 5 minutes on each side. Serve with hamburger buns, prepared mustard, ketchup, or other condiments as desired.

Makes 10 servings.

Larry and Jenny Charles
Sadieville, Kentucky
University of Kentucky Wildcat Fans

Barbecue Beef Sandwich

2 pounds ground beef
1 cup chopped onion
2 cups water
3/4 cup ketchup
2 tablespoons chili powder
2 tablespoons prepared mustard
Salt and pepper to taste

In a large skillet, brown ground beef with chopped onion until beef is no longer pink; remove to brown paper towels to drain. Pour off grease; add water, ketchup and chili powder. Bring to a boil, reduce heat, and simmer for about 6 minutes. Add cooked ground beef and onions, prepared mustard, salt and pepper. Simmer gently for about 10 minutes. Serve barbecue beef sandwiches over bulky rolls or hoagie rolls.

Marianna Marsh
Lexington, Kentucky
University of Kentucky Wildcat Fan
Paul Laurence Dunbar High School Bulldog Fan

Jumbo Party Sandwich

1/2 cup sour cream
1 tablespoon horseradish-style mustard
1/4 teaspoon salt
1/8 teaspoon black ground pepper
1 round loaf white bread, about
  2 pounds, unsliced
1 clove garlic, minced
1/4 cup butter, softened
1 tablespoon snipped Italian parsley
1 teaspoon crushed dried basil
3 cups leaf lettuce, cut into strips
6 thin slices red onion,
  separated into rings
6 ounces fontinella or
  provolone cheese, sliced
1 1/2 pounds thinly-sliced,
  cooked lean roast beef
1 red bell pepper, thinly-sliced
1/4 cup sliced pitted ripe olives

Combine sour cream, mustard, salt and pepper; reserve. Cut bread in half horizontally. Remove soft center of bread, leaving about a 1-inch-thick shell. Mash garlic; combine with butter, parsley and basil. Spread cut sides of bread with herb butter. To assemble, layer ingredients in the following order in bottom of loaf: lettuce, onion, cheese, roast beef, sour cream dressing, red pepper slices and olives. Cover with top of loaf. Cut into 8 wedges; serve immediately.

Makes 8 servings.

Bob Hilen
Lexington, Kentucky
University of Kentucky Wildcat Fan

Askews Continue Long Tradition of tailgating

Lena and Cleveland Askew, Simpsonville, have seen plenty of games in their 25-year history of tailgating. Lena said it rained so hard one game, Cleveland put her in the back of the truck where she ended up staying all day. At another game, she said they started grilling out of the back of their truck and neighboring tailgaters were asking to buy their enticing, aroma-filled goodies. Both Lena and Cleveland, also Shelby County High School Rocket fans, agree their neighboring tailgaters are wonderful, respecting everyone's parking spot and willing to help out if you run out of items. The Askews had a secret marinating sauce for chicken for this Cardinal game.

Shelby County Rockets and Louisville Cardinal fans Lena and Cleveland Askew of Simpsonville cele-brated 25 years of tailgating during the 2003 University of Louisville football season. Their specialty is marinated chicken breasts and a secret sauce they said is great.

Eastern Kentucky University fans got into some simple tailgating during a Colonels game in 2003. From left to right are Pat Smith, Harold Borders, Paint Lick, Gary Ford and his sons, Patrick and Nick, all from Richmond.

Philly Cheese Steaks

1 teaspoon olive oil
1 jumbo onion, about 12 ounces,
   thinly sliced
1 medium red bell pepper, thinly sliced
1 medium green bell pepper,
   thinly sliced
4 hero-style rolls,
   cut horizontally in half
8 ounces thinly-sliced deli roast beef
4 ounces thinly-sliced provolone cheese

These sandwiches have all the flavor of the traditional Philadelphia treat, but take half the time; while the peppers and onion cook on the stove, the broiler is working, too. In a nonstick 12-inch skillet, heat olive oil over medium-high heat until hot. Add onion and peppers, and cook about 12 minutes or until tender and golden, stirring occasionally. Meanwhile, preheat broiler. Place rolls, cut sides up, on rack in broiling pan. Top each bottom half with one-fourth of roast beef and one-fourth of cheese. With broiling pan 5 to 7 inches from source of heat, broil 1 to 2 minutes, until cheese melts and bread is toasted. Pile onion mixture on top of melted cheese; replace top halves of rolls.

Makes 4 sandwiches.

Jeff Baker
Danville, Kentucky
University of Indiana Hoosier Fan
Danville High School Admiral Fan

Grilled Chicken Sandwich

1/2 cup olive oil
2 garlic cloves, chopped
1/4 teaspoon crushed red pepper flakes
2 tablespoons chopped fresh ginger
2 tablespoons chopped fresh cilantro
2 limes, juiced
4 boneless, skinless chicken breasts
2 tablespoons butter
1 sweet onion, thinly sliced
4 sandwich rolls

In a shallow dish, combine olive oil, garlic, pepper flakes, ginger, cilantro and lime juice. Pound chicken breasts lightly until an even thickness is achieved. Place in the marinade and refrigerate 2 to 6 hours. In a sauté pan over low heat, heat butter until foamy. Add onions and cook, uncovered, for 15 to 20 minutes, until onions are golden brown and caramelized. Prepare the grill. Grill marinated chicken until done, about 6 to 8 minutes, turning once. Place on rolls, top with caramelized onions, and serve.

Makes 4 servings.

Pat "Granny" Marcum
Lexington, Kentucky
University of Kentucky Wildcat Fan
Paul Laurence High School Bulldog Fan

Peanut Butter and Banana Sandwiches

Bananas, peeled and sliced
Peanut butter
Bread

Put it together!

Keaston Brown
London, Kentucky
University of Kentucky Wildcat Fan
North Laurel High School Jaguar Fan

HEATING UP THE GRIDIRON

Steaks, Ribs
&
Other Main Dishes

Buttermilk Fried Chicken

2 whole fryers
1/2 gallon rich buttermilk
2 tablespoons table salt
1 tablespoon
   Frank's Cayenne red hot sauce
4 cups self-rising flour
2 cups white self-rising cornmeal
1 tablespoon white pepper
1 tablespoon ground thyme
1 teaspoon cinnamon
1 teaspoon Spanish paprika
8 fresh large eggs

Start by rinsing chicken and cleaning out cavity. Cut into 8 equal parts. Marinate overnight in buttermilk, 1 tablespoon of the salt, hot sauce and eggs. In a mixing bowl, combine the flour, cornmeal, remaining salt, white pepper, thyme, cinnamon and paprika. Set aside. Remove chicken from marinade one piece at a time. Roll and coat each piece well in flour. Remove, shake gently, re-dip in marinade and back into dry mixture. Coat well, shake gently. Fill a deep iron skillet half full with your favorite cooking oil; I use half real butter and half canola oil, blended. Preheat the oil to

325 degrees. Fry chicken gently and be careful when turning. You should only turn chicken one time. Your key to turning is seeking small blood pockets forming on the top. It takes approximately 20 to 25 minutes per side. Chicken is done when golden brown and clear juices come forth from within the bird.

Makes 16 pieces and feeds 8 people or you and your buddy!

Michael F. Simpson
Lexington, Kentucky
University of Kentucky Wildcat Fan

Executive Chef Michael Simpson of Lexington prepared upscale dining for UK dignitaries and their guests during a 2003 game. Around 200 guests regularly dine in the President's Room underneath Commonwealth Stadium.

Barbecue Chicken

1 large chicken
16 ounces Pepsi
1 cup favorite barbecue sauce

Skin chicken and cut into pieces. Pour Pepsi into skillet and let come to rolling boil. Turn heat down and add chicken pieces. Cook, covered, 20 minutes on each side. Uncover, pour in barbecue sauce and stir. Raise heat and cook for 15 minutes; stirring until sauce is slightly thickened.

Jerry Murphy
Lexington, Kentucky
University of Kentucky Wildcat Fan

Glazed Ham

1 medium-size picnic ham
12-ounce can lemon-lime soda
1/2 cup apple cider vinegar
2 cups packed brown sugar
1/4 cup prepared mustard
1 tablespoon whole or powdered cloves
20-ounce can crushed pineapple
Pineapple slices for garnish
Cherries for garnish

Boil ham slowly in lemon-lime soda on low to medium heat. Cook, covered, on top of stove for 2 to 2 1/2 hours. Should be very tender. In a bowl, combine vinegar, brown sugar, mustard and cloves to make a glaze. Brush ham with glaze, cover and bake at 300 degrees for 1 hour. Uncover ham and stir in pineapple. Add pineapple slices and cherries in middle. (Use toothpicks to hold in place.)

Dixiana B. Solomon
Lexington, Kentucky
University of Kentucky Wildcat Fan

Goal-Line Grilled Pork

3/4 pound pork tenderloin
Salt and freshly-ground black pepper
4 medium garlic cloves, crushed
3 tablespoons honey
2 tablespoons low-salt soy sauce
2 tablespoons Dijon mustard

Preheat grill or broiler. Remove the fat from the pork, cut the pork nearly in half lengthwise and open like a book. The pork should not be cut all the way through. Salt and pepper the pork and press the crushed garlic onto the meat on both sides. Combine the honey, soy sauce and mustard. Place pork on tray and spoon half the honey-mustard sauce over it. Broil 7 minutes. If using a grill, place pork on grill and spoon half the honey-mustard sauce over it. Grill pork 7 minutes. Remove both from grill or broiler; slice pork on an angle. Serve pork with the remaining sauce spooned over the sliced pieces.

Eddie Vandenbroek
Lexington, Kentucky
University of Kentucky Wildcat Fan

Grannie Charles' Meat Loaf

15-ounce can tomato sauce
2 to 3 pounds ground beef
3 eggs
2 sleeves saltine crackers
15-ounce can Spanish rice
1/2 cup chopped onions

Mix one-quarter of the tomato sauce with all the other ingredients. Shape into a loaf and bake at 375 degrees for 1 1/2 hours. Pour the rest of the tomato sauce over meat loaf while cooking.

Louise "Grannie" Charles
Lexington, Kentucky
University of Kentucky Wildcat Fan
Paul Laurence Dunbar High School Bulldog Fan

Patsy Todd's Chuck Roast Barbecue

2 1/2 pounds boneless chuck roast, trimmed
2 small onions, chopped
12-ounce can cola-flavored beverage
1/3 cup Worcestershire sauce
1 1/2 tablespoons apple cider vinegar or white vinegar
1 1/2 teaspoons beef bouillon granules
3/4 teaspoon dry mustard
3/4 teaspoon chili powder
1/4 to 1/2 teaspoon ground red pepper
3 garlic cloves, minced
1 cup ketchup
1 tablespoon butter or margarine

Place roast in a 3 1/2-quart electric slow cooker. Add onion. Combine cola and next seven ingredients. Cover and chill 1 cup sauce. Pour remaining sauce over roast. Cover and cook on high for 6 hours or on low for 9 hours or until roast is very tender. Using a slotted spoon, remove roast and chopped onions from cooker; shred meat with two forks. Combine reserved sauce, ketchup and butter in a saucepan. Cook over medium heat, stirring constantly until thoroughly heated. Pour sauce over shredded meat, stirring gently. Spoon meat mixture onto buns.

Makes 6 servings.

Patsy Todd
Lexington, Kentucky
University of Kentucky Wildcat Fan

Kathryn Todd, 2004 University of Kentucky graduate and daughter of UK President Lee and Patsy Todd, enjoyed visiting with UK staff member Ida Byrd during a Wildcat home game.

Rookie Ribs

3 tablespoons kosher salt
3 tablespoons black pepper
3 tablespoons paprika
3 tablespoons brown sugar
6 racks baby back ribs, 4 to 6 pounds
12 tablespoons sweet and hot rub
3 cups favorite barbecue sauce

Stir first four ingredients together in a mixing bowl. Set aside. If cooking on grill: Soak 2 cups wood chips, preferably applewood, in 2 cups apple cider or water for 1 hour; drain. Remove thin, papery skin on back of each rack of ribs or ask butcher to. (Pull if off in a sheet with your fingers, using a corner of a dish towel for a secure grip.) Sprinkle two-thirds of the rub on both sides of the ribs, patting it in with your fingers. Let rest for 30 minutes while you light the grill or preheat the oven. Set up grill. Place ribs on a rack in the center of the grill away from the heat and cook for 1 hour. Brush ribs with remaining sauce. Cook 15 to 30 minutes more. The meat will be very tender and will have pulled back from the ends of the bones. Transfer ribs to a platter. Brush with more sauce. Sprinkle with remaining rub. Serve remaining sauce on the side.

Makes 8 servings.

Chris Mefford
Lexington, Kentucky
University of Kentucky Wildcat Fan
Paul Laurence Dunbar High School Bulldog Fan

Most Spirited Tailgater

Ellen Houston turned 91 on July 1, 2004 and said she's not missed a University of Kentucky football game since 1975. Houston and her group of 30 Shriners or wives of Shriners said they have been attending Wildcat games since 1937 and have not missed a game since World War II. The group usually sets up three or four hours before a game with everyone bringing a dish. They tailgate out of vans and tents. She said many of the women now are widows so the tailgaters pick them up to attend the game each week. According to Houston, tailgating has been around as long as football has.

Kentucky Smoked Sausages

2 pounds lean turkey sausage
2 cups dry red wine
1 tablespoon fennel seeds
2 cups beer
1 onion, thinly sliced
2 pounds smoked turkey sausage
1/3 cup honey
1/2 cup orange juice

Pierce the lean turkey sausage casings in several places with the tines of a fork. Place in a bowl with the red wine and fennel. Let it sit in the refrigerator for at least 4 to 6 hours.

After marinating, place the sausage, wine and fennel in a sauté pan. Bring to a boil, reduce heat to medium-high, and cook until most of the wine is absorbed by the sausages, about 20 to 30 minutes.

Remove from heat and let cool. Pierce the casings of the smoked turkey sausage in several places with the tines of a fork. Place the sausage in a sauté pan. Add the beer and the thinly sliced onion. Bring to a boil, reduce heat to medium-high and cook until most of the beer is absorbed and the onions are very soft, approximately 20 minutes. Remove from heat and set sausages aside. Discard the onions. Turn broiler on high. Place the smoked sausage on a foil-lined broiler pan. Blend the honey and the orange juice together and brush liberally on the smoked sausages. Broil on one side until crispy, about one minute. Repeat on the other side. Remove from the heat and allow to cool. Refrigerate until ready to serve. To serve, slice each sausage link into 3 to 4 thick slices. Dip in the mustard of your choice.

Russ Williams
Lexington, Kentucky
University of Kentucky Wildcat Fan

Kentucky Bourbon Chicken

2 tablespoons olive oil
2 tablespoons Dijon mustard
1/4 cup bourbon whiskey
2 tablespoons red wine vinegar
2 tablespoons Worcestershire sauce
2 tablespoons soy sauce
1/4 cup brown sugar
2 garlic cloves, minced
Sea salt
Black pepper
1 1/2 pounds chicken breast halves, boneless and skinless

In a mixing bowl, combine all ingredients except chicken. Add chicken pieces, cover and refrigerate at least 2 hours or as long as overnight. Remove chicken from marinade. Discard marinade. Place chicken on grill over medium heat. Grill, uncovered, for 15 to 20 minutes, turning once.

Sean Marcum
Louisville, Kentucky
University of Florida 'Gator Fan

Surprise Chicken

1 large fryer, cut up
8-ounce bottle Russian salad dressing
1-ounce package onion soup mix
10-ounce jar apricot jam

Place chicken pieces in large casserole dish. Mix all other ingredients together and pour over chicken. Bake at 350 degrees for 1 1/2 hours.

Jerry Murphy
Lexington, Kentucky
University of Kentucky Wildcat Fan

Dove Breast

Dove breasts
   (as many as you have on hand)
6-ounce jar jalapeño peppers, sliced
Bacon slices, cut in half
Toothpicks
Favorite barbecue sauce
Open pit barbecue

Slice the meat from a dove breast. Place a slice of jalapeño pepper on the meat and fold. Wrap with bacon and use two toothpicks to secure. Marinate in barbecue sauce for several hours, making sure all meat is coated. Grill until bacon is crispy.

Steve and Cheryl Glenn
Frankfort, Kentucky
University of Kentucky Wildcat Fans

Debbie Dickerson, left, and daughter Alisa enjoyed tailgating for the first time last season. Son and brother Jason, #73, emerged as the starting long snapper on placekicks and punts for the University of Kentucky Wildcats in the second half of the 2003 season. Jason is a biology major and is considering medical school.

Freshman tailgaters Jane and Mike Malone enjoy their first year with 2003 Eastern Kentucky University freshman player and son, Greg. The Malones are from Centerville, KY.

BLT Steak

Two 12-ounce beef top loin steaks,
   cut 1 1/4 inches thick
8 slices bacon
1/2 cup bottled balsamic
   vinaigrette salad dressing
12 red and/or yellow tomato slices
2 cups torn mixed salad greens

Grill steaks on the rack of an uncovered grill directly over medium coals until desired doneness, turning once halfway through grilling. Allow 14 to 18 minutes for medium-rare doneness or 17 to 21 minutes for medium doneness. Meanwhile, in a skillet cook bacon until crisp. Drain bacon on paper towels, reserving 1 tablespoon drippings in skillet. Add balsamic vinaigrette salad dressing to the drippings in skillet. Cook and stir for 1 minute, scraping up any browned bits. Halve the steaks. Top steaks with tomato slices, bacon, mixed greens, and dressing mixture.

Linda Gray
Lexington, Kentucky
University of Tennessee Volunteer Fan
University of Kentucky Wildcat Fan
Paul Laurence Dunbar High School Bulldog Fan

River City Strip Steaks

2 tablespoons prepared horseradish
2 tablespoons lemon juice
4 teaspoons sugar
1 teaspoons paprika
2 teaspoons bottled minced garlic
   or 4 cloves fresh garlic
1 teaspoon salt
1 teaspoon ground black pepper
1/2 teaspoon instant
   beef bouillon granules
Four 8-ounce beef top loin steaks,
   cut 1 inch thick

In a small bowl combine horseradish, lemon juice, sugar, paprika, garlic, salt, pepper and beef bouillon granules. Trim fat from meat. Rub mixture on both sides of each steak. Cover and refrigerate for at least one hour. Grill steaks until they reach the desired doneness.

Nora Bailey
Louisville, Kentucky
University of Louisville Cardinal Fan

Spicy Maple Glazed Pork Loin

3/4 cup beer
1/4 cup maple-flavored syrup or
    mild molasses
10-ounce can chile peppers,
    finely chopped
2 tablespoons creamy peanut butter
1 tablespoon Worcestershire sauce
2 teaspoons Dijon mustard
1 teaspoon minced garlic or
    2 cloves fresh garlic
1/2 teaspoon ground cinnamon
One 4- to 5-pound pork loin center
    rib roast
1/2 teaspoon salt
1/4 teaspoon ground pepper

In a small saucepan, combine beer, syrup or molasses, chile peppers, peanut butter, Worcestershire sauce, mustard, garlic and cinnamon. Bring to a boil and then reduce heat, simmering uncovered for 30 minutes. Trim fat from meat, if necessary. Sprinkle meat with salt and pepper. Cover and grill for 2 to 2 1/2 hours, brushing meat with glaze every 20 minutes. Remove meat from grill and let stand for 10 minutes before slicing and serving.

Michael Simpson
Lexington, Kentucky
University of Kentucky Wildcat Fan

Southern Barbecue Chops

4 boneless pork top loin chops, cut
    1 to 1 1/4 inches thick
1/3 cup yellow mustard
1/3 cup red wine vinegar
5 teaspoons brown sugar
2 tablespoons butter
2 tablespoons Worcestershire sauce
1/2 teaspoon freshly-ground
    black pepper
1/4 teaspoon hot pepper sauce

In a small saucepan, whisk together mustard, vinegar, brown sugar, butter, Worcestershire sauce, black pepper, and hot pepper sauce. Bring to a boil, reduce heat, and simmer for 5 minutes. Remove from heat and cool slightly. Set aside half of the sauce to serve with chops. Brush remaining sauce on chops and grill 25 to 30 minutes.

Chris Mefford
Lexington, Kentucky
University of Kentucky Wildcat Fan
Paul Laurence Dunbar High School Bulldog Fan

Lazy Lasagna

48-ounce jar spaghetti sauce
  with meat
1 1/2 pounds ground beef
Salt and pepper to taste
1-pound box curly-shaped macaroni
16 ounces ricotta or cottage cheese
8-ounce package shredded cheese
Parmesan cheese

Heat the sauce while frying the ground beef; season the ground beef with the salt and pepper. Add the ground beef to the sauce. You may want to add Italian sausage, cut into small pieces, for extra flavor. Cook macaroni and drain. Add meat sauce, ricotta cheese and three-quarters of the shredded cheese. Stir until well blended. Pour into a 9x13-inch baking dish, topping with remaining shredded cheese and Parmesan cheese. Bake at 350 degrees for 20 minutes or until heated through. Serve with garlic bread and salad.

Judi Quire
Frankfort, Kentucky
University of Kentucky Wildcat Fan

Tailgating Tacos

5 pounds ground beef
Two 1-ounce packets taco seasoning
Two 16-ounce bottles hot taco sauce
16-ounce bag sharp Cheddar cheese
Taco shells, either hard or soft
Lettuce
8 ounces sour cream
Tomatoes

Brown ground beef and drain in pot. Add taco seasoning, sauce, and sprinkle with cheese. Let cheese melt (you may add more to taste along with extra hot sauce). Simmer for 10 minutes. Serve in shells with condiments added. For extra flavor, roll meat in soft shells and sprinkle with cheese.

Marianna Marsh
Lexington, Kentucky
University of Kentucky Wildcat Fan
Paul Laurence Dunbar High School Bulldog Fan

Pasta Pie

8 ounces uncooked spaghetti
2 tablespoons butter
1/3 cup grated Parmesan cheese
1 cup cottage cheese
1 pound lean ground beef
1/4 cup chopped green bell pepper
1/2 cup chopped onion
8-ounce can tomatoes
6-ounce can tomato paste
1 teaspoon dried oregano
1 garlic clove
1 teaspoon sugar
6 ounces shredded mozzarella cheese

Cook pasta and drain. Stir in butter and Parmesan cheese. Form crust in 10-inch pie plate by pressing pasta to bottom and sides. Sprinkle with cottage cheese. In skillet, cook meat, green pepper and onion; drain. Stir in tomatoes, tomato paste, oregano, garlic clove and sugar. Pour on crust and bake, uncovered, at 350 degrees. Sprinkle with mozzarella cheese on and bake an additional 10 minutes.

J.C. Denny
Lexington, Kentucky
University of Kentucky Wildcat Fan

Grilled Chicken and Vegetables

4 chicken breast halves, skin and
  bones removed
1/2 cup Italian salad dressing
4 potatoes, sliced
1 red bell pepper, cut into strips
1 green bell pepper, cut into strips
2 medium onions, sliced
2 tomatoes, peeled and quartered
Salt to taste
Black pepper to taste

Marinate chicken in salad dressing for 3 hours or overnight in refrigerator. Place each chicken piece on an 18x14-inch foil sheet. Add potatoes, red pepper, green pepper, onions and tomatoes to each chicken piece. Season with salt and pepper. Fold foil over ingredients and roll edges to seal, forming an envelope. Place on grill and cook for about 40 minutes or bake in oven at 350 degrees for about 50 minutes or until chicken is thoroughly cooked. Turn packets occasionally.

Louise "Grannie" Charles
Lexington, Kentucky
University of Kentucky Wildcat Fan
Paul Laurence Dunbar Bulldogs Fan

Barbecue Baby Back Ribs

4 cups wood chips (apple or hickory)
4 pounds pork loin back ribs or
    meaty spareribs
2 tablespoons barbecue seasoning
1 tablespoon garlic powder
1 teaspoon onion salt
1/2 teaspoon celery seed, crushed
1/4 teaspoon ground red pepper
1/2 to 3/4 cup bottled barbecue sauce

At least 1 hour before smoking, soak wood chips in enough water to cover. Drain before using. Trim fat from ribs. For rub, in a small bowl stir together the barbecue seasoning, garlic powder, onion salt, celery seed and red pepper. Sprinkle seasoning mixture evenly over ribs; rub in with your fingers. Preheat grill. Adjust for indirect cooking over medium heat. Add soaked wood chips according to manufacturer's directions, or wrap in foil and add to grill. Cover and heat about 10 minutes or until chips begin to smoke. Place ribs, bone sides down, in a roasting pan; set the pan on the grill rack on unlit burner, or place ribs in a rib rack and place on grill rack over unlit burner. Cover and smoke for 1 1/2 to 2 hours or until ribs are very tender. Cut ribs into serving-size pieces. Heat the barbecue sauce and pass with ribs.

Makes 6 to 8 servings.

Jackie Christenson
Florence, Kentucky
Arizona State University Sun Devil Fan

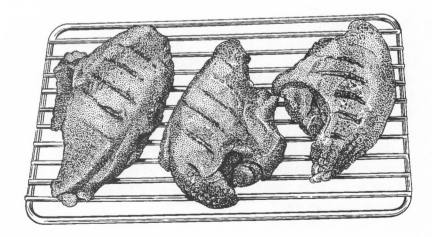

Kentucky Hog Roast

Choose a hog between 100 and 150 pounds. Get 100 pounds of charcoal. Get a hog cooker (see photo). Ask the butcher to skin it from the neck down. Most are cooked with the skin left on, but basting the pig with the special mop sauce while it's on the grill helps to tenderize the meat and adds a great flavor. When you pick the pig up, make sure and keep it cold until you're ready to cook it. About 10 bags of ice and a clean tarp work well. Stuff 2 bags of ice in the cavity, the rest around the outside, and wrap it up in the tarp. When you unwrap it, wash it off and then spray the entire hog with vegetable oil. Next, give it a good massage with the dry rub. If you are using charcoal, start with 25 pounds. Put charcoal in two piles underneath the shoulders and hams. When the coals are ready, put the hog on the grill. Place a meat thermometer in the deepest part of the ham, making sure it is not touching a bone. The bone gets hotter than the meat and will give a false reading. Put metal-framed sunglasses and a cap of the day's opponent on the pig.

Close the cooker and have a shot of good ol' Kentucky bourbon. Resist the urge to open the cooker every time someone wants to see the pig. I'm no good at this and can't say no. Try to open it only every 45 minutes. The first time you open it (after 45 minutes), wet it down good with the mop sauce. You will now start doing this every time you open it until its done. In a separate regular grill, start your charcoals that are going to be added (about once an hour). You want them hot before you shovel them in. If you keep an eye on your fire and make sure it stays hot, the cooking time for a 125-pound pig should be about 8 to 9 hours. When the temperature gauge reads 170 degrees, the ol' girl's ready. Take the remaining mop sauce and pour it into some semi-deep pans. Put the pans of sauce on the grill to keep them warm. As you carve the meat, place it in the warmed sauce. Serve the pig straight from the pan to the plate. And that's how the "Kentucky Big-Headed Boy" cooks a hog. Now if you think I am going to give my top secret mop sauce recipe away, you're crazier than me. But I will give a tame version of it and the dry rub that will make your pig cookin' a success.

Mop Sauce:

1 gallon apple cider vinegar
1/2 cup soy sauce
1 cup ketchup
1 1/2 cups packed brown sugar
5 tablespoons crushed red pepper
5 tablespoons paprika

Dry Rub:

Black pepper
Salt
Red pepper
Brown sugar
Paprika
Orange peel

Darrell Hail
Lexington, Kentucky
University of Kentucky Wildcat Fan

Darrell Hail, Lexington, checks the hog he roasted during a 2003 University of Kentucky football game against Arkansas. Hail uses his own secret ingredients for the sauce on the hog.

Kentucky Hot Brown

1/2 stick butter
1 tablespoon all-purpose flour
2 cups milk
1/2 pound Velveeta cheese
4 ounces sharp Cheddar cheese
6 slices lightly-toasted bread
6 slices baked turkey breast
6 slices baked ham, optional
Cayenne pepper
8 slices fried bacon
12 slices tomatoes

Melt butter in double boiler. Add flour and stir until there are no lumps. Add milk, stirring constantly; slowly add cheeses. Cook until thickened. In 9x13-inch buttered casserole dish, arrange lightly toasted bread and add slice of turkey and ham on each. Pour melted cheese sauce over entire casserole. Sprinkle with cayenne pepper to desired taste. Lay bacon over top of each slice of bread. Add tomatoes to each. Broil in oven until cheese browns.

Serves 6 people.

Robert Gray
Lexington, Kentucky
University of Tennessee Volunteer Fan
Paul Laurence Dunbar High School Bulldog Fan

Chicken Casserole

2 cups diced chicken
2 cups diced celery
1/2 cup toasted slivered almonds
1 cup mayonnaise
1/2 teaspoon salt
2 teaspoons grated onion
10.75-ounce can mushroom soup
2 sleeves Ritz crackers or 8.5 ounces
    potato chips, crushed

Mix together all ingredients except crackers or chips. Spread in a baking dish. Put potato chips or Ritz crackers on top. Bake 30 minutes at 350 degrees.

Serves 8 to 10.

Linda Herrington
Lexington, Kentucky
University of Kentucky Wildcat Fan

Tailgating Tacos

5 pounds ground beef or
   3 pounds chicken
1 large onion, chopped
Taco shells, either hard or soft
Two 16-ounce bottles hot taco sauce
Two 1-ounce packets taco seasoning
16-ounce package sharp
   Cheddar cheese
8-ounce package mozzarella cheese
Lettuce
8 ounces sour cream
Tomatoes

Brown ground beef or chicken and onion; drain in pot. Add taco sauce and seasoning; sprinkle with cheese. Let cheese melt (you may add more to taste along with extra hot sauce). Simmer. Serve in taco shells with shredded lettuce, sour cream and diced tomatoes.

Alyssa Oakley
Lexington, Kentucky
University of Kentucky Wildcat Fan

SEC Baby Back Ribs

2/3 cup Kikkoman teriyaki baste
   and glaze
1/3 cup beer
2 garlic cloves, minced
4 pounds pork back ribs,
   cut into serving size pieces

Blend together baste and glaze, beer and garlic. Brush ribs thoroughly with some of the baste and glaze mixture. Place half of ribs, meaty side up, in a 13x9x2-inch microwave safe baking dish. Cover; microwave on medium high for 15 minutes, turning ribs over and rotating dish after 8 minutes. Remove ribs; keep warm. Place ribs on grill 8 to 10 inches from medium-hot heat; brush with baste and glaze mixture. Grill for 8 to 10 minutes, turning over and brushing frequently.

Tammy Pickett
Russell Springs, Kentucky
University of Kentucky Wildcat Fan
Russell County High School Laker Fan

Beef Tenderloin Kabobs

1 3/4 cups soy sauce
1 cup lemon juice
1/3 cup Worcestershire sauce
1 tablespoon salt
1 tablespoon white pepper
2 teaspoons garlic powder
1 1/2 pounds beef tenderloin,
    cut into 1-inch cubes
3 medium cobs of corn,
    cut into 1-inch sections
7-ounce jar roasted peppers,
    drained and sliced
2 medium onions, diced
Vegetable oil

In a large resealable bag, combine soy sauce, lemon juice, Worcestershire and seasonings. Add beef cubes. Press air out of bag; close top securely. Turn bag over several times to coat meat. Refrigerate at least 2 1/2 hours, turning bag occasionally. Drain and discard marinade. Meanwhile, parboil corn for 5 minutes; drain. On 6 metal or soaked wooden skewers, thread beef and vegetables. Baste kabobs with oil. Grill or broil for 4 or 5 minutes on each side or until meat reaches desired doneness.

Robert Gray
Lexington, Kentucky
University of Tennessee Volunteer Fan
Paul Laurence Dunbar High School Bulldog Fan

Hawaiian Pork and Pineapple Kabobs

1 fresh pineapple, cubed
1/2 cup Litehouse stir fry sauce
1 pound marinated teriyaki pork
    tenderloin, cut into 1-inch cubes

In a small saucepan, drain juice from pineapple. Add stir fry sauce and heat until combined. Alternately thread pineapple pieces and pork onto metal skewers. Place kabobs on grill and brush with pineapple-stir fry sauce. Grill over medium-high heat for 12 to 15 minutes, turning occasionally and basting, until pork reaches 160 degrees internally.

George Cowan
Edinburgh, Scotland
Paul Laurence Dunbar High School Bulldog Fan

Affordable Fillets

1 pound lean ground beef
Salt to taste
Pepper to taste
1/4 cup grated Parmesan cheese
2-ounce can mushroom stems
    and pieces, drained
3 tablespoons finely-chopped
    pimento stuffed olives
2 tablespoons finely-chopped onion
2 tablespoons finely-chopped
    green bell pepper
5 slices bacon,
    partially cooked and drained

Pat ground beef on waxed paper into a 12x7x1/4-inch rectangular casserole dish. Sprinkle lightly with salt and pepper. Top with cheese. Combine mushrooms, olives, onions, and green peppers and sprinkle over meat. Roll up meat in jelly roll fashion, starting with the short end. Cut into 1 1/2 inch slices. Wrap edge of each slice with bacon, securing with wooden picks. Broil or grill to desired doneness.

Linda Herrington
Lexington, Kentucky
University of Kentucky Wildcat Fan

Beefy Cheese Casserole

1 pound ground beef
1/2 cup chopped onion
1/2 cup chopped celery
8-ounce can tomato sauce
10.75-ounce can mushrooms, drained
Salt and pepper
7-ounce package macaroni, cooked
1 cup shredded Cheddar cheese

Brown beef, onion and celery. Stir in tomato sauce and mushrooms. Season with salt and pepper. Combine with macaroni and pour into 2-quart casserole dish. Top with Cheddar cheese. Bake at 350 degrees for 25 minutes.

Jerry Murphy
Lexington, Kentucky
University of Kentucky Wildcat Fan

Breakfast Casserole

1 pound sausage
3 eggs
1 1/2 cups milk
2 cups shredded Cheddar cheese
2 cups bread crumbs

Brown sausage and drain. In a mixing bowl, mix eggs and milk together. Grease a 9x13-inch casserole dish. Combine egg/milk mixture with bread crumbs and sausage; salt lightly. Stir in half of the cheese. Pour into the casserole dish and cover with remaining cheese. Bake at 350 degrees for 60 to 70 minutes. Casserole can be doubled easily.

Carol Ann Maupin
Lexington, Kentucky
University of Kentucky Wildcat Fan

Chicken Pot Pie

10.75-ounce can cream of chicken soup
10.75-ounce can cream of potato soup
15-ounce can mixed vegetables
10-ounce can white chicken chunks
15-ounce box Pillsbury pie crusts

Mix soups, vegetables and chicken chunks together. Pour into unbaked pie crust, covering with second crust and bake at 400 degrees for 1 hour.

Don Witt
Lexington, Kentucky
University of Kentucky Wildcat Fan

Sausage Casserole

1 pound mild pork sausage
1 onion, chopped
1 green bell pepper, chopped
1/2 cup chopped celery
1 cup cooked rice
10.75-ounce can cream of chicken soup
8-ounce can mushrooms, drained
2-ounce jar pimentos,
    chopped and drained
1 cup shredded sharp Cheddar cheese

Place sausage in 8x12-inch baking dish. Microwave at high for 6 to 7 minutes, stirring well after 3 minutes. Add onion, green pepper and celery. Microwave at high 3 to 5 minutes. Drain off excess drippings. Stir rice into sausage mixture. Add soup, mushrooms and pimentos. Cover with waxed paper. Microwave at high 5 to 7 minutes. Uncover, sprinkle cheese on top, re-cover and microwave at high for 1 to 2 minutes.

Jerry Murphy
Lexington, Kentucky
University of Kentucky Wildcat Fan

Outback Bowl Tailgater Sings the Blues!

Vern Miracle and his wife went to Tampa for the Outback Bowl and arrived on New Year's Eve. They found a place to park their RV on a corner across from the stadium. It was cold that night. His wife had gone inside and he had drinks around a lit barbecue grill in the parking lot with other visitors. Some of the guys decided to go to a local strip club and he stayed with the main group. After awhile, one of the club visitors came back singing the blues! He had supposedly been talking to one of the strippers and heard a distant voice calling his name. He had pulled his cellular phone out of an inner jacket pocket and his wife was on it talking to him. He had called her earlier and had somehow hit "last call" and "send" and his wife heard him talking to the stripper. He said she wanted to have a "serious talk" when he got home. Vern had just met these guys so he's not sure what happened later.

Neither Rain, Sleet Nor Snow Could Stop EKU Tailgaters

Some tailgaters have been around long enough to remember when men had to wear ties and women had to "dress up" to attend an Eastern Kentucky University football game. For the past seven years, however, this group of 12 Richmond, Kentucky residents and EKU graduates has worn all the correct gear to weather sleet, snow, and rain. According to Dee Riggs, their love for the Colonels and EKU is the common thread that keeps them coming back to tailgate every year. "We used to tailgate after games and football players came by," said Riggs. "It's been so much fun and we really look forward to it." The rivalries, according to the group, have given them memories they love to share. "One year," laughed Joe Blankenship, "Morehead (State University) sprayed the visitor's bleachers down with water to clean them before the game. They froze and were so slick, we didn't think we'd ever be able to get up the steps!" Some of these stories, according to Neil Parke, just make the "best thing about the good ol' days is, they're gone!" The Richmond tailgaters include Judy and Fred Dodd, Dorothy and Neil Parke, Brenda and Joe Blankenship, Phillis and Michael Adams, Dee and Jay Riggs, Francis Roberts and Erman Wintz.

A seven-year-old tailgate club, this group of former players, coaches, employees and graduates of Eastern Kentucky University would show up in Richmond no matter what type of weather was forecast. The group includes, front row, left to right, Judy Dodd, Dorothy Parke, Brenda Blankenship, Phillis Adams, Michael Adams; back row, left to right, Fred Dodd, Neil Parke, Jay Riggs, Dee Riggs, Joe Blankenship, Francis Roberts and Erman Wintz.

OFF SIDES

Veggies, Taters

&

Other Side Dishes

Best in the SEC Barbecue Bean Bake

1 pound ground beef
1 pound bacon, chopped
1 onion, chopped
1/2 cup ketchup
1/2 cup barbecue sauce
1 teaspoon salt
1 teaspoon chili powder
4 tablespoons prepared mustard
3/4 teaspoon pepper
1/4 cup brown sugar, optional
Two 16-ounce cans red kidney beans
Two 16-ounce cans pork and beans
Two 16-ounce cans butter beans

In a large pot such as a Dutch oven, brown the ground beef, bacon and onion. Drain excess fat. Combine and add all other ingredients except the beans; stir well. Add beans and combine thoroughly. Bake for 1 hour at 350 degrees.

Serves 20.

Gene Oakley
Lexington, Kentucky
University of Kentucky Wildcat Fan
Paul Laurence Dunbar High School Bulldog Fan

Corn Pudding

15-ounce can cream style corn
2 heaping tablespoons all-purpose flour
3/4 cup sugar
3 eggs
1 cup whipping cream, not whipped
1/2 cup milk

Grease a 2-quart casserole dish. Put corn in dish. In a small bowl, mix flour and sugar together. In a separate bowl, beat eggs, then stir in cream and milk. Add the flour mixture. Pour and stir into corn. Dot the top of the casserole with butter. Bake at 350 degrees for 1 hour.

Carol Ann Maupin
Lexington, Kentucky
University of Kentucky Wildcat Fan

Corn Pudding

Two 15-ounce cans cream corn
14-ounce can sweetened
    condensed milk
4 tablespoons all-purpose flour
4 eggs, beaten
1 teaspoon salt
Butter

Combine all ingredients except butter. Pour into a 2-quart baking dish and put pats of butter on top. Bake at 350 degrees for 1 hour.

Don Witt
Lexington, Kentucky
University of Kentucky Wildcat Fan

Marinated Asparagus

30 asparagus spears
8-ounce bottle Zesty Italian dressing
3 to 4 leaves romaine lettuce
Yellow, green, red bell peppers, chopped
Cherry tomatoes
2 to 3 green onions, chopped
2 hard-boiled eggs
3-ounce bottle real bacon bits

Cook asparagus 3 to 4 minutes. Drain. Place in flat container with lid. Pour dressing over hot asparagus. Cover and refrigerate 24 hours. To serve, drain asparagus and place on lettuce leaves. Top with peppers, tomatoes, onions, eggs and bacon bits.

Diana Burke
Lexington, Kentucky
University of Kentucky Wildcat Fan
Scott County High School Cardinal Fan

Tailgate Hummus

15-ounce cans garbanzo beans,
   undrained
3 to 4 garlic cloves
1/4 cup plus 1 tablespoon tahini, also
   called sesame seed paste
3 tablespoons water
3 tablespoons olive oil

Drain garbanzo beans, reserving 1/4 cup liquid, and set aside. Position knife blade in food processor bowl. Drop garlic through food chute with processor running and process 3 seconds or until minced. Add garbanzo beans, reserved 1/4 cup liquid and remaining ingredients. Process 3 minutes or until smooth. If you don't have a food processor, you can use a blender; just mince the garlic beforehand. Spoon mixture into a serving bowl. Serve with pita bread and raw vegetables.

Sherrie Fleckinstein
Lexington, Kentucky
University of Kentucky Wildcat Fan

Fried Corn

Bacon slices, fried and chopped
Two 15.25-ounce cans
   sweet corn kernels, drained
1 teaspoon sugar
1 teaspoon butter
Salt and pepper to taste

Make this in an iron skillet, if possible. Fry bacon until crisp and remove from skillet to drain. Add corn, sugar and butter to drippings in skillet; add salt and pepper. Crumble bacon back into the skillet. Cover and simmer for about 30 minutes on medium heat. You can add whole frozen green beans to this if you like.

Lisha Popplewell
Russell Springs, Kentucky
University of Kentucky Wildcat Fan
Russell County High School Laker Fan

A University of Louisville fan shows his true spirit.

If you visit the parking lot during a University of Louisville football game, you will see lots of red and black vehicles sporting their best wishes.

Lots O' Beans

Two 15-ounce cans pork and beans
15-ounce can lima beans
15.5-ounce can kidney beans
15-ounce can Great Northern beans
2 large chopped onions, preferably
    Vidalia, chopped
Butter for sautéing
1/2 cup brown sugar
2 teaspoons brown mustard
1/3 cup cider vinegar
1/2 pound bacon

Put beans in large casserole dish. In a saucepan, sauté onions with butter. Add brown sugar, mustard and vinegar to onions. Stir, then pour over beans. Arrange bacon slices on top and bake at 350 degrees for 1 hour.

Caroline Preston
Catlettsburg, Kentucky
Lawrence County High School Bulldog Fan

Best Ever Potatoes

7 cups coarsely-chopped
    small red potatoes
1 cup chopped onion
8-ounce carton sour cream
1 cup shredded Monterey Jack cheese
1 cup shredded sharp Cheddar cheese
1/2 teaspoon salt
1/4 teaspoon cayenne pepper
2 medium tomatoes, chopped

Cook potatoes and onion in water a large covered saucepan for 12 to 14 minutes or until tender; drain. Stir in the sour cream, Monterey Jack cheese, Cheddar cheese, salt and cayenne pepper. Stir in the tomatoes. Spoon mixture into a 2-quart rectangular baking dish and bake, uncovered, at 350 degrees for 30 minutes.

Coach Judy Cox
Lexington, Kentucky
University of Kentucky Wildcat Fan
Paris High School Lady Hound Fan

Potato Casserole

2 pounds frozen, cubed potatoes
10 3/4-ounce can cream chicken soup
8 ounces sour cream
1 medium onion, chopped
16-ounce package shredded cheese
1 stick butter
2 cups cornflakes, crushed

Combine first five ingredients in a mixing bowl and spoon into a 9x13-inch casserole dish. Melt butter and mix with crushed cornflakes; sprinkle on top of casserole. Bake at 350 degrees for 45 minutes.

Beth Oakley
Lexington, Kentucky
University of Kentucky Wildcat Fan

Broccoli Corn Bread

Two 8.5-ounce packages
    Jiffy corn bread mix
10-ounce box frozen chopped broccoli, thawed
16-ounce carton cottage cheese
4 eggs, beaten
1 1/2 sticks butter, melted

Combine corn bread mix, broccoli, cottage cheese and eggs. Mix well. Pour melted butter into 9x13-inch pan. Pour butter over mixture. Bake at 375 degrees for 45 minutes.

Linda Herrington
Lexington, Kentucky
University of Kentucky Wildcat Fan

Iron Skillet Corn Bread

3 to 4 tablespoons cooking oil
2 cups self-rising cornmeal
1 egg
1 1/2 cups buttermilk
2 heaping tablespoons mayonnaise

Heat oven to 400 degrees. Pour 3 to 4 tablespoons oil into skillet. In a mixing bowl, combine cornmeal, egg, buttermilk and mayonnaise and pour into skillet. Bake 15 to 20 minutes or until golden brown. Cut into wedges to serve.

Linda Herrington
Lexington, Kentucky
University of Kentucky Wildcat Fan

Long Bomb Broccoli Casserole

1 family-size bag frozen broccoli, chopped
1 1/2 sticks butter
4 heaping tablespoons all-purpose flour
2 cups milk
1 cup chicken bouillon
1 1/2 pounds Velveeta cheese
1 stick butter
2 sleeves Ritz crackers, crumbled

Steam broccoli. Melt butter in medium saucepan. Stir in flour until creamy. Add milk and bouillon. Stir until thick consistency; if needed, add 1 more tablespoon flour. Gradually add cheese and cook until completely melted. Pour drained broccoli into 9x13-inch casserole dish. Pour cheese sauce over broccoli. In medium glass bowl, melt butter and add crumbled crackers, mixing well. Sprinkle cracker mixture over casserole. Bake in 350-degree oven for 15 to 20 minutes.

The late Clema "Brownie" "Memmaw" White
Lexington, Kentucky
University of Kentucky Wildcat Fan

Easy Red Beans and Rice

1 onion
1 pound smoked Polish sausage
Green bell pepper, as desired
32-ounce container salsa
Two 12-ounce cans red kidney beans
Cajun spice to taste

Chop onion and smoked sausage and sauté with green pepper if using. Add salsa , kidney beans and Cajun spice. Any brand of salsa can be used, I like medium hot.

Vern Miracle
Lexington, Kentucky
University of Kentucky Wildcat Fan

Hash Brown Casserole

5.2-ounce box
   Betty Crocker hash browns
1 cup hot water
10 3/4-ounce Campbell's
   cream of chicken or cream of
   celery soup, undiluted
1 medium yellow onion, diced
8-ounce bag Velveeta shredded cheese
2 tablespoons margarine

In large bowl, combine hash browns and hot water. Let soak until moist. Drain the water off the potatoes. Add soup, diced onion and Velveeta cheese; stir. Add margarine and stir again. Bake in 400-degree oven until golden brown on top. Best if casserole sits 5 to 10 minutes before serving.

Sherry Vice
Lexington, Kentucky
University of Kentucky Wildcat Fan

Louisville Fans Love Camaraderie

Eleanor Montgomery and Joann Smith remember the old Louisville Fairgrounds where their favorite Cardinal team used to play before moving to Papa John's Cardinal Stadium a few years ago. Even though the group of seven have braved some severe weather and even fought off pneumonia, they say the camaraderie brings them back each year…and the food, which includes deep fried fish and gumbo, deep fried turkey, white chili and regular chili, breakfast sausage biscuits and gravy, fried apple pies and fried potatoes. The group also cheers for DeSales, Central and Moore High Schools and said they would tailgate for basketball if they could figure out a way. The group includes Eleanor, Joann, William Montgomery, Eva Bradley, Jim Bradley, Naomi Hannon and Riley Hannon, all of Louisville.

Posing for a group shot are University of Louisville die-hard fans, seated, left to right, Eleanor Montgomery and William Montgomery; back row, left to right, Joann Smith, Eva Bradley, Jim Bradley, Naomi Hannon and Riley Hannon. The group has been tailgating since 1983.

Kidd Begins Rookie Tailgate Season

"Rookie tailgater" Roy Kidd, fourth from left, spent his first season off the football field in 39 years. The Eastern Kentucky University football coach and legend spent his first season tailgating with some special "All-Americans" he coached in 1968. From left to right are Jim Clark (Richmond, KY), Jim Moberly (Richmond, KY), Jim Guice (Coral Springs, FL), Coach Kidd, Ron House (Richmond, KY), Cope Guice (Margate, FL) and Sheila Sturgill (Richmond, KY).

Sausage Muffins

1 pound sausage
2 cups Bisquick
10 3/4-ounce can Cheddar cheese soup
1/2 cup water
16-ounce package shredded
   Cheddar cheese

Cook sausage; drain and crumble. In a mixing bowl, combine sausage, Bisquick, soup, water and cheese; mix well. Fill mini muffin tins 3/4 full. Bake at 375 degrees for 15 to 20 minutes.

Jordan Baker
Lexington, Kentucky
University of Kentucky Wildcat Fan

Kicker Quiche

9-inch pie shell, unbaked
1 large egg
1/2 cup mayonnaise
1/2 cup evaporated milk
1 tablespoon cornstarch
Salt to taste
Pepper to taste
1 cup shredded ham
1 1/2 cups shredded Swiss cheese
1 medium onion, chopped

Bake pie shell at 425 degrees for 7 to 8 minutes. In a mixing bowl, whip the egg, mayonnaise, milk, cornstarch, salt and pepper. Fill pie shell; bake at 350 degrees for 40 to 45 minutes. Let stand 10 minutes before cutting into pie slices.

Cheri Freeman
Lexington, Kentucky
University of Kentucky Wildcat Fan

Spicy SEC Slices

1 1/2 pounds small russet potatoes,
  cut lengthwise into 1/4-inch-thick
  slices
2 teaspoons olive oil
1 teaspoon chili powder
1/4 teaspoon salt

Place potatoes in a large bowl or resealable plastic bag and coat with oil; sprinkle with chili powder and salt. Preheat grill to medium-high and arrange potatoes in a single layer; turn as necessary.

Heidi Maynard
Lexington, Kentucky
University of Kentucky Wildcat Fan

Barbecued New Potatoes

22 small new potatoes,
  evenly sized if possible
1/4 to 1/2 cup quality olive oil
6 cloves of garlic
12 sprigs fresh thyme
4 pieces aluminum foil, squared
2 tablespoons coarse salt or
  sea salt
Water

Wash and dry new potatoes. Rub olive oil on potatoes. Put a clove of garlic and two sprigs of fresh thyme on each square of foil. Arrange 6 new potatoes on each square, sprinkle with coarse salt and seal in packets, leaving a small opening in each. Sprinkle a tablespoon of water into each packet and seal the openings. Place the foil packets over a medium-heat grill and cook until tender, which depends on the size of the potatoes. Turn the packets every few minutes.

Bob and Jenny Morehouse
Lexington, Kentucky
University of Kentucky Wildcat Fan

Green Bean Casserole

Two 16-ounce cans whole green beans, drained
1/2 cup French dressing
1/2 cup chopped onions
6 to 9 strips bacon, cooked and crumbled

Combine first three ingredients and place in a 9x13-inch casserole dish. Sprinkle with bacon and bake 30 minutes at 350 degrees.

Kim Novicki
Louisville, Kentucky
University of Kentucky Wildcat Fan

Parsley New Potatoes

Two 16-ounce cans sliced new potatoes, drained
1/4 cup margarine, melted
1/4 cup chopped fresh parsley
Salt and pepper to taste

Place new potatoes in a 9x13-inch casserole dish. Mix margarine and parsley and pour over potatoes. Season with salt and pepper to taste. Bake 20 minutes at 350 degrees.

Larry Richardson
Nicholasville, Kentucky
University of Kentucky Wildcat Fan
Harrison County High School Thoroughbred Fan

Blow Out Baked Beans

2 to 3 slices bacon
1 onion, chopped
15-ounce can pork and beans
1/4 cup ketchup
2 to 3 tablespoons brown sugar
Dash of mustard
Dash of Worcestershire sauce
Dash of salt

Fry bacon, set aside and drain fat. Cook onion in grease from bacon. Add all other ingredients except bacon. Stir mixture over low heat. Pour into a 9x13-inch casserole dish. Sprinkle with crumbled bacon. Bake 20 to 25 minutes in oven at 375 degrees.

The late Clema "Brownie" "Memmaw" White
Lexington, Kentucky
University of Kentucky Wildcat Fan

Monday Night Macaroni and Cheese

16-ounce box elbow macaroni
1 stick butter
2 cups milk
1 1/2 pounds Velveeta cheese
Salt and pepper to taste

Cook macaroni and drain. Add butter, milk and cheese. Mix well and add salt and pepper to taste.

Sherry Vice
Lexington, Kentucky
University of Kentucky Wildcat Fan

EKU Parents "Life-Long" Friends & Tailgaters

When the Kuehnes and Moberlys started tailgating, they were already one up on the other Eastern Kentucky University tailgaters because Ed Kuehne and Jim Moberly had already been part of the Colonel family, playing for Coach Roy Kidd in the '60s. This year, these tailgaters have converted a horse trailer into a tailgate wagon, complete with everything a tailgater would need! The foursome have been tailgating since 1979 and said it's been fun to continue their EKU Colonel traditions.

From left to right, Ed and Paula Kuehne, the Colonel mascot, and Billie and Jim Moberly pose in front of a horse trailer they use for tailgating. Ed and Jim played for Coach Roy Kidd in the '60s and have remained friends tailgating since 1979.

Long Distance Fan Supports the 'Cats

While he manages to see at least one Wildcat football game a year, Gary Bartoo says he has absolutely no connection to the Bluegrass except for his love of the "Big Blue." A graduate of Temple University and a Penn State University fan, Bartoo said he also became a basketball fan and quickly fell in love with the Wildcat hoopsters. "I've always followed basketball and you can't love basketball and not know about UK." Once he retired his post as principal in 1997, the South Wales, New York resident decided it was time to reserve his seats at Commonwealth Stadium. "There's a great atmosphere here for football fans," said Bartoo, "and I try to plan a trip as often as I can. Kentucky is just a great state for college sports."

South Wales, New York native Gary Bartoo, said there is no better fan base than that of the University of Kentucky. Bartoo is a Temple graduate and Penn State fan but says he loves UK and manages to travel to the Bluegrass State at least twice during the season for football and basketball.

HOW SWEET IT IS!

Cakes, Cookies

&

Other Sweet Treats

Big Ol' Cookies

2 cups butter, melted
2 cups brown sugar
2 cups sugar
4 eggs, beaten
2 teaspoons vanilla extract
4 cups all-purpose flour
2 teaspoons baking soda
2 teaspoons baking powder
1 cup old-fashioned oats
2 cups cornflakes, crushed
2 cups chocolate chips
1 cup raisins
1 cup shredded coconut

In a mixing bowl, blend melted butter, brown sugar, sugar, eggs and vanilla extract. Stir the flour, baking soda and baking powder; add to butter-sugar mixture. Add remaining ingredients to mixture and blend. Place spoonfuls of dough on an ungreased cookie sheet and bake for 12 minutes at 350 degrees. Cookies will spread while baking.

Makes 6 dozen large cookies.

Karen Brooks
Lexington, Kentucky
University of Kentucky Wildcat Fan

Bourbon Balls

2/3 cup chopped pecans
1/3 cup bourbon
1/2 cup margarine, melted
16-ounce bag confectioners' sugar
12-ounce bag semisweet
   chocolate chips
4 ounces paraffin

Soak nuts in bourbon for one hour. In a mixing bowl, combine melted margarine and sugar. Add bourbon and nuts. Roll into small balls and refrigerate for 2 hours. When bourbon balls have set, melt chocolate chips and paraffin in double broiler. Dip balls into chocolate mixture. Refrigerate until chocolate is firm.

Don Witt
Lexington, Kentucky
University of Kentucky Wildcat Fan

Easy Texas Sheet Cake

Cake:

2 sticks butter
1 cup water
4 tablespoons unsweetened
   cocoa powder
2 cups sugar
2 cups all-purpose flour
1/3 teaspoon salt
1/2 cup milk with 1 teaspoon
   baking soda dissolved in it
1 teaspoon vanilla extract
2 eggs

Frosting:

1 stick butter
4 tablespoons unsweetened
   cocoa powder
6 tablespoons milk
16-ounce box confectioners' sugar
1 teaspoon vanilla extract
1 cup chopped nuts, chopped

To make the cake, combine butter, water and cocoa powder in a large saucepan and bring to a boil. Remove from the heat and add the sugar, flour, salt, milk/baking soda, vanilla extract and eggs. Beat well. Pour onto a large jelly roll pan and bake at 350 degrees for 20 minutes. When the cake has baked for 15 minutes, start making the frosting: Place butter, cocoa and milk in a saucepan and bring to a boil. Remove from the heat and stir in confectioners' sugar, vanilla extract and milk. Spread on cake while both are still hot.

Ida Byrd
Lexington, Kentucky
University of Kentucky Wildcat Fan
Tates Creek High School Commodore Fan

Chocolate Peanut Treats

3/4 cup graham cracker crumbs
1/2 cup margarine, melted
2 cups confectioners' sugar
1/2 cup chunky peanut butter
6 ounces semisweet chocolate chips

In a bowl, combine cracker crumbs and margarine; mix well. Stir in sugar and peanut butter. Press into a greased 8-inch square pan. In a microwave or double boiler, melt the chips, stirring until smooth. Spread over peanut butter layer. Chill for 30 minutes. Cut into squares. Chill until firm, about 30 minutes longer. Store in refrigerator.

Josh Oakley
Lexington, Kentucky
University of Kentucky Wildcat Fan
University of Georgia Bulldog Fan
Paul Laurence Dunbar High School Bulldog Fan

Triple Crown Pie

1 cup sugar
1 cup all-purpose flour
1 stick butter, melted and cooled
2 eggs, well beaten
1 teaspoon vanilla extract
1 cup chocolate chips
1 cup pecans, broken or whole
9-inch unbaked pie shell

Preheat oven to 350 degrees. Mix sugar and flour together; set aside. Combine cooled butter with eggs. Stir in vanilla and flour-sugar mixture; mix well. Stir in chocolate chips and nuts. Pour into unbaked pie shell Bake at 350 degrees for 30 to 40 minutes or until center is set. Cool, slice and serve; top with whipped cream, if desired.

Don Witt
Lexington, Kentucky
University of Kentucky Wildcat Fan

Special tailgaters come out in fashion to cheer on the University of Louisville Cardinals. One such guest was Star Wars celebrity "Yoda," who came complete with red and black Cardinal apparel.

Like any good mascot, the University of Louisville "Cardinal" took time to pose for the camera before working the crowd of tailgaters getting ready for a 2003 UL football game.

Dirt Cake

20-ounce bag Oreo cookies
1/4 cup butter
1 cup confectioners' sugar
8-ounce package cream cheese
Two 3 1/2-ounce packages
   French vanilla instant pudding
8-ounce container frozen whipped
   topping, thawed

Reserve filling from centers of 3 or 4 Oreo cookies, place in a small dish and refrigerate. Crush all the cookies in a large plastic bag using a rolling pin, or in a food processor. Cream together the butter, confectioners' sugar and cream cheese. In another bowl, mix together the milk, instant pudding and thawed whipped topping. Combine cream cheese mixture and pudding mixture, blending well. Alternate layers of the mixture and the cookie crumbs in a clean black plastic flowerpot, starting and ending with the cookie crumbs. Refrigerate. Before serving, crumble reserved white Oreo filling on top to resemble fertilizer.

Ryan Oakley
Lexington, Kentucky
University of Tennessee Volunteer Fan
Paul Laurence Dunbar High School Bulldog Fan

Fudge Sundae Pie

1/4 teaspoon salt
1 cup evaporated milk
6 ounce package chocolate chips
1 cup miniature marshmallows
Vanilla wafers
Vanilla ice cream

Combine salt, milk, chocolate chips and marshmallows in pan. Cook over medium heat until chocolate chips and marshmallows melt. Continue to stir until the mixture thickens, about 2 minutes. Line bottom of 9-inch pie pan with vanilla wafers. Slice vanilla ice cream and use to make a layer on top of the vanilla wafers; cover ice cream with half of the chocolate mixture. Repeat layers — vanilla wafers, ice cream, chocolate mixture. Freeze for 2 to 5 hours. This recipe can easily be doubled.

Phyllis Nash
Lexington, Kentucky
University of Kentucky Wildcat Fan

Go Big Blueberry Crumble

1 cup zwieback toast crumbs
1/4 cup sugar
3 tablespoons butter
2 cups fresh blueberries

Combine crumbs and sugar. Cut in butter until well mixed. Place 1 cup blueberries in 10x10- inch baking dish and cover with half of the butter-crumb mix. Repeat layers. Bake at 350 degrees about 30 minutes. Especially good still warm with a bit of ice cream!

Makes 6 servings.

John and Jo Greene
Lexington, Kentucky
University of Kentucky Wildcat Fans

Mound Cake

18.25-ounce package
    chocolate cake mix
1 stick butter, softened
1 cup evaporated milk
3/4 cup sugar
24 large marshmallows
14-ounce package coconut flakes
12-ounce package chocolate chips
1 stick butter

Prepare cake mix according to package directions. Add the stick of softened butter. Bake in a greased and floured 17x11 1/2 -inch jelly roll pan for 15 minutes. Be careful, it will burn easy! Combine next four ingredients in heavy sauce pan and beat until marshmallows are melted. Spread over cake. Melt next two ingredients in heavy pan over low heat. Spread over coconut layer. Refrigerate.

Kathy Mullins
Lexington, Kentucky
University of Kentucky Wildcat Fan

Neiman Marcus Bars

18.25-ounce box
    butter pecan cake mix
3 eggs
1 stick butter, melted
8 ounces cream cheese
1 stick butter
1 pound powdered sugar
1 cup chopped pecans

Combine cake mix, one of the eggs, and melted butter. Pour into a 9x13-inch baking dish. In a mixing bowl, blend the cream cheese, butter, remaining two eggs and powdered sugar. Pour over the cake mix layer. Sprinkle pecans on top and bake in a preheated 350-degree oven for 1 hour. Cool before cutting into small squares.

Becky Naugle
Lexington, Kentucky
University of Kentucky Wildcat Fan

Old-Fashioned Coconut Cream Pie

1/2 cup all-purpose flour
3/4 cup white sugar
1/4 teaspoon salt
3 cups half-and-half
2 egg yolks, beaten
1 cup flaked coconut, toasted
1 teaspoon vanilla extract
9-inch pie crust, baked
3 cups frozen whipped topping, thawed

In a heavy, medium-size saucepan, combine flour, sugar and salt. Gradually stir in half and half. Bring to a boil over medium heat, stirring constantly for 5 minutes. Remove pan from heat. Place egg yolk mixture back into half and half mixture. Cook over low heat for 3 minutes. Stir in 1/2 cup coconut and vanilla. Cover and cool. Spoon cooled filling into baked crust. Cover with plastic wrap and chill thoroughly. Before serving, top with whipped topping and remaining 1/2 cup toasted coconut.

Makes 8 servings.

Jennifer Dunlap
Lexington, Kentucky
University of Kentucky Wildcat Fan

Peanut Butter Bars

1/2 cup butter, at room temperature
1/2 cup brown sugar
1/2 cup white sugar
1 egg
1/3 cup peanut butter
1/2 teaspoon baking soda
1/2 teaspoon vanilla extract
1/4 teaspoon salt
1 cup all-purpose flour
1 cup old-fashioned oats
1 cup chocolate chips
1/2 cup powdered sugar
2 to 3 tablespoons milk
1/4 cup peanut butter

In a mixing bowl, blend the butter, brown sugar and white sugar. Beat in the egg, 1/3 cup peanut butter, baking soda, vanilla extract, salt, flour and oats. Spread in a 9x13-inch pan and bake at 350 degrees for 15 to 20 minutes in a preheated oven. Sprinkle chocolate chips over the hot bars and spread when melted. In a bowl, combine powdered sugar, milk and 1/4 cup peanut butter. Drizzle over the chocolate. Cut into bars.

Becky Naugle
Lexington, Kentucky
University of Kentucky Wildcat Fan

Pecan Tassies

1/2 cup butter or margarine, softened
3-ounce package cream cheese
1 cup all-purpose flour

Filling:

1 egg, beaten
3/4 cup brown sugar
1 teaspoon butter, softened
1 teaspoon vanilla extract
Pinch salt
2/3 cup pecans, chopped

Blend 1/2 cup softened butter, cream cheese and flour until smooth. Shape into 1-inch balls and press into small muffin tins. For the filling, blend the egg, brown sugar, 1 teaspoon softened butter, vanilla extract and salt. Stir in pecans. Pour filling into muffin tins. Bake at 350 degrees for 30 to 40 minutes.

Makes 18 to 24.

Wini Humphrey
Lexington, Kentucky
University of Kentucky Wildcat Fan

Tom Teague, right, gives grilling lessons to future tailgater and grandson Dylan Logan. Both are from Hazard. Teague said he cooks most of the morning on the day of an afternoon game at the University of Kentucky. Dylan, on the other hand, was more interested in the finished product than actually doing the cooking.

Tom Teague, Hazard, entices his neighbors by grilling early so that he won't miss any of the University of Kentucky Wildcats football game.

Sandra and Henry Alliston, Westport, have been traveling from Conyers, GA to tailgate during their son's football games with the Colonels at Eastern Kentucky University in Richmond. Their son, Matt, was a junior in 2003. The Allistons missed only one game that year and only two since Matt has been playing.

Pound Cake

3 cups all-purpose flour
1/2 teaspoon baking powder
1/2 teaspoon salt
1 cup butter, softened
3 cups sugar
5 eggs
1/2 cup shortening
1 cup milk
1/2 teaspoon vanilla extract

Sift flour, baking powder and salt in a bowl. Place butter and sugar in a mixing bowl; cream until light and fluffy. Add eggs, one at a time; beat thoroughly between after each. If an electric mixer is used, do not stop mixer while adding eggs. Add milk and vanilla extract. Add half the sifted flour mixture. Beat about 1 minute. Add remaining flour mixture. Beat about 1 minute. Use rubber spatula to collect all flour from sides of mixing bowl. Pour into greased and floured tube cake pan. Bake for 1 hour to 1 hour and 20 minutes at 325 degrees, checking for doneness periodically. Remove from pan immediately after removing from oven. Cool on a cake rack.

Malaby Byrd
Lexington, Kentucky
University of Kentucky Wildcat Fan
Tates Creek High School Commodore Fan

Praline Apple Pie

1 apple pie, homemade or
  store-bought
1/2 stick or 1/4 cup butter
1 cup brown sugar, packed
1/3 cup whipping cream
1 teaspoon vanilla extract
1 cup powdered sugar
3/4 cup pecans or pecan halves,
  chopped

Bake the apple pie; cool for 1 hour. In a 2-quart saucepan, bring butter, brown sugar and whipping cream to a boil in a 2-quart saucepan over medium heat, stirring often. Boil 1 minute and remove from heat. Whisk in vanilla extract and powdered sugar until smooth. Pour mixture slowly over pie, spreading to cover. Sprinkle with pecans.

Therese Logan
Elkmont, Alabama
University of Kentucky Wildcat Fan

Rocky Road Fudge Brownies

19.8-ounce package brownie mix
1 cup chopped pecans
3 cups miniature marshmallows
Two 1-ounce squares
    unsweetened chocolate
1/3 cup milk,
    plus a little extra if needed
1/2 cup butter or margarine
16-ounce package powdered
    sugar, sifted
1 teaspoon vanilla extract

Prepare brownie mix according to package directions; stir in pecans. Spoon batter into a greased 13x9x2-inch baking pan. Bake at 350 degrees for 25 minutes.

Remove from oven and sprinkle miniature marshmallows over hot brownies. Combine chocolate, milk and butter in a heavy saucepan. Cook over low heat until chocolate and butter melt, stirring often. Remove from heat. Transfer to a medium mixing bowl. Add powdered sugar and vanilla; beat at low speed with an electric mixer until smooth. (If frosting is too stiff for spreading consistency, add more milk, 1 tablespoon at a time, stirring until smooth.) Spread over brownies. Cool in pan on a wire rack and cut into bars.

Makes 1 dozen.

Dr. Lee Todd, President
University of Kentucky
Lexington, Kentucky
University of Kentucky Wildcat Fan

Rich 'N' Easy Chocolate Mousse

3 eggs
1/4 cup sugar
12 ounces semisweet
  chocolate morsels
2 tablespoons brandy or rum
1 cup hot milk
Whipped cream to garnish

In electric blender, combine eggs, sugar, chocolate morsels and rum. (I blend the eggs first to a frothy stage before adding the other items.) Heat milk just to the boiling point. Pour milk slowly into blender with the motor running. Cover and blend on medium speed until chocolate is melted and mixture is smooth. Pour into 8 pot de crème or demitasse cups. Chill until set. Serve garnished with whipped cream. May also be poured into a chocolate crumb pie crust. Refrigerate until ready to serve.

Josephine Walker
Lexington, Kentucky
University of Kentucky Wildcat Fan

Six Layer Dessert

1 stick margarine
1 cup all-purpose flour
1 cup chopped nuts
1 cup sugar
8 ounces cream cheese
16 ounces prepared whipped topping
6 ounces instant vanilla pudding
3 cups milk
6 ounces instant chocolate pudding
1.45-ounce Hershey bar

Melt margarine in 9x13-inch pan. Add flour and mix well. Add nuts. Bake 15 minutes at 350 degrees. Let cool. In a mixing bowl, blend the sugar, cream cheese and half of the prepared whipped topping. Spread on crust. Mix vanilla pudding with 1 1/2 cups of the milk. Beat until thick. Spread on second layer. Mix chocolate pudding with remaining 1 1/2 cups milk. Beat until thick. Spread on vanilla pudding layer. Spread remaining whipped topping over chocolate pudding layer. Grate Hershey bar over the top. Refrigerate overnight.

Don Witt
Lexington, Kentucky
University of Kentucky Wildcat Fan

Rum Cake

Margarine for greasing cake pan
1 cup chopped pecans
3-ounce box vanilla pudding,
   not instant
1 box butter recipe golden cake mix,
     not butter fudge
1/2 cup light rum
1/2 cup water
1/2 cup vegetable oil
4 eggs

Hot glaze:

1 stick margarine
1 cup sugar
1/4 cup light rum
3/4 cup water

Grease an angel food cake pan or bundt cake pan with margarine. Mix chopped nuts and vanilla pudding and sprinkle on bottom of cake pan. Lightly mix cake mix, rum, water and oil. Add eggs one at a time until well blended. Pour carefully into pan so as not to disturb the nuts.

Bake at 325 degrees for 50 to 60 minutes. Test cake with a toothpick; if it comes out dry, cake is done. Remove cake from oven. Loosen around edges and center tube with table knife. To make the hot glaze, combine margarine, sugar, rum and water in a saucepan. Boil 3 minutes. Pour over hot cake. Glaze will run down and around cake where it has been loosened by knife. Be sure cake has cooled before removing from pan so as not to crumble. (I cover it with Reynolds Wrap and poke holes in the foil so as to let some of the steam escape and leave it sitting overnight.) After cake is cooled, loosen around edges and center tube once again and turn upside down onto a cake plate. If some of the nuts stick, just spoon them out and place on top of cake. If using 2 mini bundt pans, fill half full and bake at 325 degrees for about 30 to 40 minutes.

Don and Peggi Frazier
Lexington, Kentucky
University of Kentucky Wildcat Fans

Pineapple Upside-Down Cake

1/4 cup butter or margarine, melted
20-ounce can sliced pineapples
10 pecan halves
12-ounce jar apricot preserves
18 1/4-ounce package yellow cake mix

Pour melted butter into a well-greased 13x9x2-inch baking dish. Drain pineapple, reserving 1/4 cup juice. Arrange pineapple slices in prepared pan; place a pecan half in the center of each slice. Combine the apricot preserves and reserved pineapple juice; spoon over pineapple slices. Prepare cake batter according to package directions; pour over pineapple. Bake at 350 degrees for 45 to 50 minutes or until toothpick inserted near the center comes out clean.

The late Sam Mays
Lexington, Kentucky
University of Kentucky Wildcat Fan

Peanut Butter Cake

1 stick margarine
1/2 cup water
3/4 cup peanut butter
1/2 cup oil
2 cups all-purpose flour, sifted
2 cups sugar
2 eggs, slightly beaten
1 teaspoon vanilla extract
1/2 cup milk
1 teaspoon baking soda

Icing:

1 stick butter
1/3 cup milk
1/2 cup peanut butter
1 teaspoon vanilla extract
Powdered sugar

In a saucepan, bring margarine, water, 3/4 cup peanut butter and oil to a boil. Remove from heat and add flour, sugar, eggs, vanilla extract, milk and baking soda; stir until well blended. Pour into greased and floured oblong pan. Bake at 350 degrees for 35 minutes. For the icing, place butter, milk and 1/2 cup peanut butter in a saucepan; bring to a boil. Remove from heat and add vanilla and powdered sugar, stirring until smooth.

Linda Herrington
Lexington, Kentucky
University of Kentucky Wildcat Fan

Linda's Butter Pound Cake

4 sticks margarine or butter
2 3/4 cups sugar
9 eggs
3 1/2 cups sifted all-purpose flour
1/4 teaspoon cream of tartar
1 tablespoon vanilla extract
1 tablespoon lemon extract

Cream butter and sugar for 7 minutes with electric mixer. Add eggs one at a time, beating 3 minutes after each addition. Add flour, cream of tartar and extracts. Pour into tube pan that has been greased and floured. Bake at 300 degrees for 1 1/4 to 1 1/2 hours.

Linda Herrington
Lexington, Kentucky
University of Kentucky Wildcat Fan

Pumpkin Cake

4 eggs
1 cup oil
2 cups sugar
2 cups pumpkin
2 teaspoons cinnamon
1/2 teaspoon nutmeg
1/4 teaspoon allspice
1/4 teaspoon ginger
2 cups self-rising flour
1 teaspoon baking soda

Icing:

1 stick butter
1 teaspoon vanilla extract
16-ounce box powdered sugar
3 ounces cream cheese

In a mixing bowl, cream together the eggs, oil and sugar. Blend in the pumpkin. In a separate bowl, sift together the spices, flour and baking soda; add to pumpkin mixture. Bake 30 to 40 minutes at 350 degrees in oblong cake pan. For the icing, blend the butter, vanilla, powdered sugar and cream cheese. Use to frost cake.

Linda Herrington
Lexington, Kentucky
University of Kentucky Wildcat Fan

While they follow the red and white of their favorite high school team and hometown, the Scott County (Georgetown, Kentucky) Cardinals, these "true blue" fans dress accordingly to tailgate for the University of Kentucky. Seated is Harry Dickerson, standing, left to right, are George Lockard, Linda Dickerson and Patsy Rich.

Football season takes in a few holidays, and a University of Kentucky fan, Joe Richardson, got creative during Halloween, decorating a pumpkin for the "ghostly" occasion.

Eastern Kentucky University football tailgaters took a break from eating and socializing long enough to have their photos taken.

Clem's Date Balls

3/4 cup sugar
1 stick butter
2 egg yolks, beaten
1 cup chopped pecans
2 tablespoons marshmallow creme
1 teaspoon vanilla extract
2 cups crisped rice cereal
Confectioners' sugar for
　coating date balls
1 package chopped dates

Mix sugar, butter, egg yolks, pecans and marshmallow creme on low heat, stirring, for 5 to 10 minutes. Stir in vanilla extract and cereal. Fold in dates. Roll into small balls and coat in confectioners' sugar.

Linda Herrington
Lexington, Kentucky
University of Kentucky Wildcat Fan

Chocolate Cream Cupcakes

8-ounce package cream cheese,
　softened
1 egg, slightly beaten
1/2 cup sugar
1 cup chocolate chips
18.25-ounce box devil's food cake mix

In a mixing bowl, combine cream cheese, egg and sugar. Stir in chocolate chips. In a separate bowl, prepare devil's food cake batter according to directions on package. Spoon cake mixture into 2-inch cupcake papers. Add 1 teaspoon of marshmallow creme mixture in center and press in slightly. Bake at 350 degrees for 18 minutes.

The late Sam Mays
Lexington, Kentucky
University of Kentucky Wildcat Fan

Irresistible Brownies

1 1/2 sticks margarine
2 cups sugar
1 1/2 cups all-purpose flour
1/2 cup unsweetened cocoa powder
1/2 teaspoon baking powder
1/4 teaspoon salt
4 eggs
2 teaspoons vanilla extract
1/2 cup chopped nuts, optional
1 cup chocolate chips

Melt margarine on low heat. Add sugar, flour, cocoa, baking powder, salt, eggs and vanilla extract. Stir in nuts if using. Stir all until well blended. Spread in greased 13x9-inch pan. Sprinkle chocolate chips on top. Bake 30 to 35 minutes at 350 degrees.

Lois Newkirk Williams
Lexington, Kentucky
University of Kentucky Wildcat Fan

Chocolate Chip Blonde Brownies

2 cups all-purpose flour
1 teaspoon baking powder
1/4 teaspoon baking soda
1 teaspoon salt
1 cup chopped nuts
2/3 cup margarine
2 cups firmly-packed brown sugar
2 eggs, slightly beaten
2 teaspoons vanilla extract
1 package semisweet chocolate chips

In a large mixing bowl, combine first 5 ingredients well and set aside. In large saucepan, melt margarine. Remove from heat. Add brown sugar, eggs and vanilla extract. Mix well. Gradually add small amounts of dry ingredients, mixing well after each addition. Spread in greased 13x9x2-inch pan. Sprinkle chips on top. Bake at 350 degrees for 25 to 30 minutes or until sides pull away from edge of pan. Middle will be set, but not hard.

Betty Howell
Lexington, Kentucky
University of Kentucky Wildcat Fan

One of Mom's Jam Cakes

1 cup buttermilk
1 cup raisins
1 cup butter, softened
2 1/2 cups sugar
6 eggs, slightly beaten
1 teaspoon baking soda
3 1/2 cups all-purpose flour
1 teaspoon ground cloves
1 teaspoon allspice
1 teaspoon cinnamon
1 cup blackberry jam
1 cup strawberry preserves
1 cup chopped walnuts

Spray loaf pans, bundt pan, round pans or cupcake pans with nonstick spray. Place buttermilk and raisins in blender and puree; set aside. In a mixing bowl, blend butter and sugar. Add eggs. Add baking soda to buttermilk/raisin mixture. In a large bowl, sift together the dry ingredients. Gradually add dry ingredients alternating with buttermilk/raisin mixture and sugar/butter/eggs mixture. Add jams and nuts to mixture. Pour into baking pans and bake at 350 degrees approximately 1 hour, or 20 minutes per cupcake. Test for doneness. Cool and store in tight tins in cool area up to 1 week.

Refrigerate/freeze if longer storage is desired.

The late Sam Mays
Lexington, Kentucky
University of Kentucky Wildcat Fan

Wildcat Caramel Brownies

18.25-ounce package
   German chocolate cake mix
3/4 cup melted butter or margarine
1/3 cup evaporated milk, undiluted
1 cup chopped nuts, optional
4 ounces caramel fruit dip, warmed
   in microwave so it's pourable
1 cup chocolate chips or
   mini chocolate chips, optional

Combine dry cake mix, butter, milk and nuts. Stir by hand until dough holds together. Press one half of dough into a 9x13-inch greased and floured pan. Bake at 350 degrees for six minutes. Remove from oven and let set a minute or two. Pour/spread caramel fruit dip on top; make sure it's pretty soft, or if you try to spread it will tear up your brownies. Sprinkle chocolate chips over caramel. Press remaining dough over the chocolate chips.

Tip:

I find the best way to do this is to take an egg-sized ball of batter — it sets up really fast — in my hand and flatten it like I'm making a hamburger and place it on top of caramel/chips. Continue until you use all of the batter; there will be small spaces between batter. Bake 15 to 18 minutes more. It may appear that it is not thoroughly cooked, but once it cools, it will be soft and chewy. Cut into small squares. I have made with and without chocolate chips, and we liked it just as well both ways. Enjoy!

Roxanne
Lexington, Kentucky
Tailgating Mom of the K-State Wildcats

Famous for his chicken legs on the grill, Stan Beeler, center, and his wife, Luria, right, from Winchester, have been avid Eastern Kentucky University tailgaters since high school. Joining the two are Kyra Hughes, a member of the OWLS organization, Older Wiser Learners.

OWLS Cheer for Colonels

In 1990, students were NUTS for Eastern Kentucky University…Not your Usual Traditional Students, that is. Fifty-three members and a name change later, these OWLS, the name they currently go by, are considered your "Older, Wiser Learners." No matter what you call them, these nontraditional students, 25 years old and above, are people who began their college education later in life. "Many of us," said OWL student Luria Beeler, Winchester, Kentucky, "started our working careers right out of high school and decided to wait until we were ready to continue our education." These OWLS get together and tailgate during the Colonels' home games. "It's a camaraderie for this group as students both in the classroom and as part of the whole university setting," said Beeler.

The proud OWLS organization promoted their cause while tailgating at an 2003 Eastern Kentucky University football game.

Kick the Can Ice Cream

4-ounce package instant pudding,
  any flavor
2 quarts whole milk
1 cup sugar
2 cans sweetened condensed milk,
Three empty 1-pound coffee cans
1 roll duct tape
Three empty 3-pound coffee cans
10 pounds ice
3 cups rock salt

Mix pudding and whole milk. Add sugar and condensed milk. Divide batter among the three 1-pound coffee cans, leaving one inch of space at the top. Put tops on cans and fasten securely with duct tape. Put one 1-pound can into each 3-pound can and add ice to fill; add 1 cup rock salt per can. Put lids on top of coffee cans and secure with duct tape. It takes approximately one half an hour of throwing the can around, rolling it on the ground or playing a game of kick the can with these to make ice cream. You might consider avoiding the inebriated player and the wannabe team return punter.

Jim and Janice Lewis
Lexington, Kentucky
University of Kentucky Wildcat Fans

Strawberry Delight

1 angel food cake
1.3-ounce box instant vanilla pudding
2 cups milk
8-ounce carton prepared
   whipped topping
12.75-ounce bottle strawberry glaze
1 quart strawberries, fresh

Break the angel food cake into small pieces and place in a Tupperware container. In a mixing bowl, combine pudding mix and milk; mix in whipped topping. Pour over cake crumbles. Squeeze glaze over all and place a few sliced strawberries around on top.

Betty J. Rose
Lexington, Kentucky
Everyone's Fan

Lou's Peanut Butter Fudge

6 cups sugar, preferably Domino
12-ounce can evaporated milk
1 cup liquid Coffee-Mate
1/2 cup butter or oleo
18-ounce jar peanut butter
16-ounce package
   Reese's peanut butter chips
16-ounce jar marshmallow creme
2 teaspoons vanilla extract

In a saucepan, mix sugar, evaporated milk, Coffee Mate and butter. Boil until mixture reaches soft ball stage – 234 to 240 degrees – on a candy thermometer. Take off heat. Mix in peanut butter, peanut butter chips, marshmallow creme and vanilla extract. Stir until well blended. Pour into greased large cake pan. Cool, cut into squares. Enjoy!

Lou J. Borders
Louisa, Kentucky
University of Louisville Cardinal fan
Lawrence County High School Bulldog Fan

Petrino's Athletic Supporters bus keeps tailgaters happy with music and fun during a University of Louisville football game.

Tailgaters come in all types of groups, including businesses, at many games. The University of Louisville had tailgaters of all levels in parking lots throughout Papa John's Cardinal Stadium.

Monster Cookies

1 pound softened butter
3 pounds crunchy peanut butter,
   about 6 1/4 cups
2 pounds brown sugar, or 4 cups
4 cups sugar
1 tablespoon corn syrup
1 tablespoon vanilla extract
8 teaspoons baking soda
12 eggs
18 cups rolled oats
Two 12-ounce bags chocolate chips
Two 16-ounce bags plain M & M's

Combine butter and peanut butter. Slowly add both brown sugar and sugar until blended well. Add corn syrup, vanilla, baking soda and eggs and stir. Slowly add oats, chocolate chips and M & M's until blended well. Drop into balls onto greased cookie sheet. Bake at 350 degrees for 10 to 13 minutes.

Jackie Christenson
Florence, Kentucky
Arizona State University Sun Devil Fan

Peanut Butter Fudge

2 cups white sugar
2/3 cups milk
1 teaspoon vinegar
1 cup peanut butter
1 cup marshmallow creme
1 teaspoon vanilla extract

Mix sugar, milk and vinegar. Bring to a boil and cook 6 minutes. Remove from heat and add peanut butter, marshmallow creme and vanilla extract. Beat and pour into greased 8-inch or 9-inch square pan. Cut into squares while still warm.

Linda Herrington
Lexington, Kentucky
University of Kentucky Wildcat Fan

Chocolate Chip Cheese Ball

8 ounces cream cheese
3/4 cup confectioners' sugar
1/2 cup real butter, melted
2 tablespoons brown sugar
1 tablespoon vanilla extract
3/4 cup miniature chocolate chips
3/4 cup chopped pecans

Soften cream cheese. Beat with confectioners' sugar, butter, brown sugar and vanilla extract until smooth. Mix in chocolate chips and 1/2 cup of the pecans. Refrigerate until firm. Shape into ball and roll in remaining pecans. Serve with graham crackers, butter cookies or pretzels.

Sandy Hilen
Lexington, Kentucky
University of Kentucky Wildcat Fan

Rice Krispie Bars

1/2 cup sugar
1/2 cup light corn syrup
1 teaspoon vanilla extract
3/4 cup creamy peanut butter
4 cups Rice Krispies
2 cups milk chocolate chips or
    1 cup milk chocolate and
    1 cup butterscotch chips

Butter 9x9-inch pan. Mix sugar and corn syrup until it reaches the boiling stage. Remove from heat. Stir in vanilla extract and peanut butter; mix well. Pour over cereal; mix well. Press into buttered pan. Melt chips and pour over cereal.

Ellen Houston
Lexington, Kentucky
University of Kentucky Wildcat Fan

First Down Fudge Brownie Pie

2 eggs
1 cup sugar
1/2 cup butter, melted
1/2 cup flour
1/3 cup unsweetened cocoa powder
1/4 teaspoon salt
1 teaspoon vanilla extract
1/2 cup chopped nuts, optional
Powdered sugar for dusting, optional

Heat oven to 350 degrees. Lightly grease 8-inch pie pan. Beat the eggs in a small mixing bowl. Blend in sugar and melted butter. Combine flour, cocoa and salt. Add to butter mixture. Stir in vanilla extract and nuts. Pour batter into pan and bake for 25 to 30 minutes or until the center is set. Cool. Cut into wedges and sprinkle with powdered sugar if desired.

Josh Oakley
Lexington, Kentucky
University of Georgia Bulldog Fan
University of Kentucky Wildcat Fan
Paul Laurence Dunbar High School Bulldog Fan

JC Denney, Lexington, has been tailgating for 15 years. He retired a few years ago, sold his home and bought a condominium and his first recreational vehicle. Denney said he loves tailgating at the University of Kentucky and makes a "popular" spaghetti pie.

CHEER-LITERS

Punch, Mixers

&

Sippers

Banana Crush

1 large ripe banana, cut in 1-inch slices
2 cups pineapple juice
1 cup ginger ale

Combine banana and pineapple juice in container and blend for 15 seconds until smooth. Add ginger ale and blend a few seconds more and serve.

Jerry Murphy
Lexington, Kentucky
University of Kentucky Wildcat Fan

Breakfast Blizzard

15-ounce can fruit cocktail
1 cup plain or vanilla yogurt
1 cup orange juice
1 ripe banana
6 to 8 ounces ice cubes

In blender combine undrained fruit, yogurt, juice, banana and ice. Blend until smooth.

Don Witt
Lexington, Kentucky
University of Kentucky Wildcat Fan

Brown Sugar Cocoa

3 ounces unsweetened chocolate
1/3 cup water
4 cups hot milk
3/4 cup brown sugar, packed
1/8 teaspoon salt

In a double boiler, melt the chocolate and water together. Slowly mix in milk, sugar and salt. Whisk until smooth and blended. Add more brown sugar for a sweeter hot chocolate mix recipe.

Louise "Grannie" Charles
Lexington, Kentucky
University of Kentucky Wildcat Fan
Paul Laurence Dunbar High School Bulldog Fan

Fruit Punch

1 1/2 cups water
3 1/2 cups sugar
3 tea bags
1 quart orange juice
1 pint lemon juice
1 quarts ice water
4 1/2 quarts pineapple juice
2 quarts ginger ale

Boil water and sugar until sugar dissolves. Let cool. Add all other ingredients, except ginger ale. Just before serving, add ginger ale.

Serves 50 or more.

Jerry Murphy
Lexington, Kentucky
University of Kentucky Wildcat Fan

Fruit Punch Delight

Four 12-ounce cans frozen
    orange juice, thawed
Three 12-ounce cans frozen lemonade,
    thawed
Two 12-ounce cans frozen limeade,
    thawed
46-ounce can pineapple juice
Three 2-liter bottles ginger ale

In a very large punch bowl, place all
ingredients with twelve 12-ounce juice
cans of water. Stir well, add ice cubes and
serve.

Jerry Murphy
Lexington, Kentucky
University of Kentucky Wildcat Fan

Hot Fruit Punch

3 cinnamon sticks
1 tablespoon whole cloves
11/2 teaspoons whole allspice
2 1/4 cups pineapple juice
2 cups cranberry juice
1 3/4 cups water
1/2 cup brown sugar, packed
1/8 teaspoon salt

In a coffee pot basket of a glass percolator, place the cinnamon sticks, cloves and
allspice. In the percolator, stir together
the pineapple juice, cranberry juice,
water, brown sugar and salt until sugar is
dissolved. Place the percolator, covered,
over medium-high heat and bring to a
boil. Perk for 5 minutes. Serve hot.

Alec Dunlap
Lexington, Kentucky
University of Kentucky Wildcat Fan

Jackie Cornett, Whitesburg, and Linda Perkins, Lexington, relaxed during an afternoon of tailgating at the University of Kentucky.

Betty Browning, left, of Lancaster, KY, and Joyce Hackett, of Bethlehem, KY, enjoy bringing food to UK Wildcat games. They say eating is the best part of the game!

Eastern Kentucky University Colonel fans Dianna and John Flanagan have been tailgating ever since the Colonel Club was established. Both from Richmond, John was also a member of the faculty at EKU.

Orange-Banana Shake

2 cups orange juice
2 large bananas, cut into 2-inch slices
1 cup vanilla ice cream

Place in blender in the order listed. Blend on high for 15 to 25 seconds and serve.

Jerry Murphy
Lexington, Kentucky
University of Kentucky Wildcat Fan

Spring Apple Punch

3 cups apple juice
1/4 cup lemon juice
1 1/2 cups apricot nectar
1/4 cup grenadine
3/4 cup ginger ale
1 pint lemon sherbet
Mint leaves for garnish

Combine apple juice, lemon juice, apricot nectar and grenadine in container and blend for 3 seconds. Fill punch bowl with ice; pour juice mixture and ginger ale into bowl. Float scoops of lemon sherbet on the surface. Garnish with mint leaves.

Jerry Murphy
Lexington, Kentucky
University of Kentucky Wildcat Fan

Tailgate Beer

1 cooler
3 bags ice (cubes)
1 case beer

Remove cans from recyclable cardboard holder. Place cans in cooler, intermingling with ice cubes. Chill 45 minutes and serve.

Anonymous
University of Kentucky Wildcat Fan

Cran-Strawberry Cooler

1 1/3 cups cranberry juice
2/3 cup white grape juice
10 fresh strawberries, divided
4 ice cubes
1 teaspoon sugar, optional

In a blender, combine juices, six strawberries, ice and, if desired, sugar; cover and process until smooth. Garnish with remaining strawberries.

Beth Oakley
Lexington, Kentucky
University of Kentucky Wildcat Fan

While the parking lots fill up around Commonwealth Stadium at the University of Kentucky, there's also dining going on below the stands. The President and his wife invite opposing team presidents, as well as local and state dignitaries, to join them for lunch with 200 or so special guests.

Newcomers to tailgating, Rena Exler, Radcliff, and Scott Stephens, Richmond, enjoy setting up their grill for a 2003 Eastern Kentucky University football outing.

Rick and Gayle Rickert bought their first RV in 2003 and named it after their beloved pooch, Sugar. Everyone wanted to "dog-sit" Sugar while the Rickerts were away so they just decided to buy their own RV and bring Sugar along. While Sugar wears the blue and white, Rick cheers for the University of Louisville and Gayle's loyalties are to the University of Kentucky.

Banana Punch

4 cups sugar
6 cups water
6 bananas
Juice of 6 lemons
6-ounce can orange juice concentrate
18-ounce can pineapple juice
1 gallon ginger ale

Mix sugar and water. Boil for 4 minutes. Cool. Combine bananas and lemon juice and puree in blender. Add orange juice concentrate and pineapple juice. Combine with sugar water mixture and freeze in gallon container. Thaw 2 hours before serving. Add chilled ginger ale.

The late Sam Mays
Lexington, Kentucky
University of Kentucky Wildcat Fan

Second Half Spicy Bloody Mary

2 to 5 dried whole chipotle peppers
1 fresh horseradish root, peeled and
    cut into medium-size julienne strips
1 tablespoon celery seed
1 tablespoon black peppercorns
Zest of one lemon or lime
Vodka

Combine peppers, horseradish, celery seed, peppercorns and zest. Pour enough vodka over ingredients to cover them. The more vodka, the milder the heat. Let sit in a cool, dark place for at least one week, shaking it up ever few days. As you use the vodka, pour in plain vodka to replace it. If you started out with a strong batch, you should be able to refill with vodka a few times until it gets too weak. Then start over. Serve as needed!

Jessica Smith
Lexington, Kentucky
West Virginia University Mountaineer Fan

Orange Slush Supreme

Two 6-ounce cans frozen lemonade,
   thawed
6-ounce can frozen orange juice,
   thawed
2 cups sugar
7 cups water
2 cups strong tea; 4 tea bags
   brewed in 2 cups water
1 cup whiskey

Mix all ingredients together and freeze.

Sara Bailey
Avon, Indiana
University of Kentucky Wildcat Fan
Paul Laurence Dunbar High School Bulldog Fan

Hometeam Kahlua

3 cups water
3 1/2 cups sugar
4 rounded tablespoons
   instant coffee granules
1 vanilla bean
1 pint water
1 pint grain alcohol

Mix water and sugar and boil 10 to 20
minutes. Add instant coffee and vanilla
bean that has been split in half lengthwise. Cool; add water and grain alcohol.
Let sit 2 weeks with vanilla bean in liquid,
then remove bean.

Walter Marcum
Lancaster, Kentucky
University of Kentucky Wildcat Fan
Paul Laurence Dunbar High School Bulldog Fan

Fresh Fruit Pudding Milk Mixers

4 cups milk
4-serving-size package vanilla flavor
   instant pudding and pie filling, or
   any flavor
1 medium ripe banana, mashed
1/2 cup finely-chopped strawberries

Place all ingredients in a large pitcher with tight-fitting lid; cover. Shake vigorously 1 minute or until well blended. Pour into 4 glasses. Serve immediately. Mixture thickens as it stands. Thin with additional milk if desired.

Makes 4 servings.

Sara Bailey
Avon, Indiana
University of Kentucky Wildcat Fan
Paul Laurence Dunbar High School Bulldog Fan

Southern Sweet Tea

6 cups water
4 family-size tea bags
1 to 1 3/4 cups sugar

Bring water to a boil in a saucepan; add tea bags. Boil 1 minute; remove from heat. Cover and steep 10 minutes. Remove tea bags, squeezing gently. Add sugar, stirring until dissolved. Pour into a 1-gallon pitcher and add enough water to fill pitcher. Serve over ice.

Makes 1 gallon.

Louise "Grannie" Charles
Lexington, Kentucky
University of Kentucky Wildcat Fan
Paul Laurence Dunbar High School Bulldog Fan

Loaded Lemonade

1/2 cup fresh orange juice
1/2 cup sweet and sour mix
1/2 cup tequila
1/2 cup orange liqueur
2 cups lemon-lime soft drink

Stir together first 4 ingredients; chill 2 hours. Stir in soft drink. Serve over ice.

Makes 4 cups.

Shannon Mullins
Lexington, Kentucky
University of Kentucky Wildcat Fan

Raspberry Tea Cooler

6 cups cranberry juice drink
2/3 cup sugar
10 regular size raspberry tea bags

Bring cranberry juice drink and sugar to a boil, stirring until sugar dissolves. Pour over tea bags, cover and steep 20 minutes; discard tea bags. Pour into a 13x9-inch pan. Freeze 8 hours. Remove from freezer 20 minutes before serving. Break into pieces and serve immediately in glasses.

Makes 6 cups.

Judy Spillman
Bucklin, Kansas
University of Kentucky Wildcat Fan

Spring Training Lemonade

6 cups white grape juice, chilled
12-ounce can frozen lemonade
    concentrate, thawed and undiluted
5 1/2 cups club soda, chilled

Stir together all ingredients in a 1-gallon pitcher or punch bowl. Serve over ice.

Amber Baker
Danville, Kentucky
University of Kentucky Wildcat Fan
Boyle County High School Rebel Fan

Hot Coffee Float

3/4 cup or 6 ounces hot,
    freshly-brewed Maxwell House or
    Yuban Coffee, any variety
1 scoop coffee, chocolate or
    vanilla ice cream

Pour coffee over ice cream in large cup or mug. Serve immediately.

Makes 1 serving.

Linda Gray
Lexington, Kentucky
University of Kentucky Wildcat Fan
University of Tennessee Volunteer Fan
Paul Laurence Dunbar High School Bulldog Fan

Hash Marks

*I*n football, when the ball carrier is either tackled or pushed out of bounds, officials return the ball in bounds to the closest hash mark to where it's spotted. Likewise, for all those tailgate chefs who want exact measurements instead of just guessing or "getting close," the following tables should help.

2 Tablespoons	= 1 Fluid Ounce
3 Tablespoons	= 1 1/2 Fluid Ounces
1/4 Cup	= 2 Fluid Ounces
1/3 Cup	= 2 1/2 Fluid Ounces
1/3 Cup + 1 Tablespoon	= 3 Fluid Ounces
1/3 Cup + 2 Tablespoons	= 3 1/2 Fluid Ounces
1/2 Cup	= 4 Fluid Ounces
2/3 Cup	= 5 Fluid Ounces
3/4 Cup	= 6 Fluid Ounces
3/4 Cup + 2 Tablespoons	= 7 Fluid Ounces
1 Cup	= 8 Fluid Ounces
1 Cup + 2 Tablespoons	= 9 Fluid Ounces
1 1/4 Cups	= 10 Fluid Ounces
1 1/3 Cups	= 11 Fluid Ounces
1 1/2 Cups	= 12 Fluid Ounces
1 2/3 Cups	= 13 Fluid Ounces
1 3/4 Cups	= 14 Fluid Ounces
1 3/4 Cups + 2 Tablespoons	= 15 Fluid Ounces
2 Cups or 1 Pint	= 16 Fluid Ounces
2 1/2 Cups	= 20 Fluid Ounces
3 3/4 Cups	= 1 1/2 Pints
4 Cups	= 1 3/4 Pints

Quantities to Serve 100 People

Coffee	3 pounds
Milk	6 gallons
Tomato Juice	4 No. 10 cans (52 cups)
Soup	5 gallons
Hot Dogs	25 pounds
Ham	40 pounds
Beef	40 pounds
Hamburger	30 to 38 pounds
Potatoes	35 pounds
Spaghetti	5 gallons
Baked Beans	5 gallons
Slaw	16 pounds
Bread	10 loaves
Rolls	200
Butter	3 pounds
Potato Salad	3 1/2 to 4 gallons
Fruit Salad	20 quarts
Cakes	8
Ice Cream	4 gallons

The Game Rosters...Game Chefs

Announcing the Talegate Team Lineups:

From Elkmont, Alabama:
    Therese Logan

From Avon, Indiana:
    Sara Bailey

From Catlettsburg, Kentucky:
    Caroline Preston

From Danville, Kentucky:
    Debbie Baker
    Jeff Baker
    Amber Baker

From Florence, Kentucky:
    Jackie Christenson

From Frankfort, Kentucky:
    Judi Quire

From Lancaster, Kentucky:
    Betty Browning
    Walter Marcum

From Lexington, Kentucky:
    Jane and Lou Adams
    Deborah I. Back
    Jordan Baker
    Karen Brooks
    Diane Burke
    Ida Byrd

Malaby Byrd
Jennifer Calvert
Jeanne and Ben Carr
Louise "Grannie" Charles
Coach Joe Pat Covington
Judy Cox
J.C. Denny
Carol Pitts Diedrichs
Alec Dunlap
Jennifer Dunlap
Marie Dunlap
Sherri Fleckinstein
Richard Ford
Don and Peggy Frazier
Cheri Freeman
Mr. and Mrs. Carl Gorham
Linda "Grandma" Gray
Robert Gray
John and Jo Greene
Rita Griffith
Helen Hague
Darrell Hall
Tammy Hatton
Laura Hayes
Robyn Hayes
Linda Herrington
Bob Hilen
Sandy Hilen
Bryan Houck
Ellen Houston
Betty Howell
Joanne Hughes
Wini Humphrey

Big John Jelley
Ingrid Judi
Karina Karakulova
Jim and Janice Lewis
Gary Link
Jimmie and Marilyn Lockhart
Mary Jo Manley
Charlie Marcum
Pat Marcum
Marianna Marsh
Carol Ann Maupin
Heidi Maynard
Sam Mays
Chris Mefford
Rachel Mefford
Vern Miracle
Bob and Jenny Morehouse
Kathy Mullins
Shannon Mullins
Jerry Murphy
Becky Naugle
Phyllis Nash
Sylvia Nutter
Alyssa Oakley
Coach Eddie Oakley
Gene "Grandaddy" and Linda
"Granny" Oakley
Jayna Oakley
Josh Oakley
Kelli Oakley
Nathan Oakley
Rodney and Beth Oakley
Ryan Oakley
Chef Jim Olert
Marilyn and Pete Owens
Ann Hughes Powell

Betty Rose
Roxanne
Michael Simpson
Jessica Smith
Dixiana Solomon
Judy Spillman
Nancy Stallard
Seth Stallard
Dr. Lee Todd
Patsy Todd
Sherry Vice
Eddie and Laura Vandenbroek
Bob Ward
Linda Watson
Josephine Walker
Clema "Brownie"
    "Memmaw" White
Lois Newkirk Williams
Russ Williams
Don Witt
Diane Young

From London, Kentucky:
    Coach Daniel and Jorene Brown
    Keaston Brown

From Louisa, Kentucky:
    Lou J. Borders

From Louisville, Kentucky:
    Nora Bailey
    Melinda Hurst
    Sean Marcum
    Kim Novicki

From Nicholasville, Kentucky:

Larry Richardson

From Russell Springs, Kentucky:
    Shaun Coffey
    Lisha Popplewell
    Tammy Pickett

From Sadieville, Kentucky:
    Larry and Jenny Charles

From Stamping Ground, Kentucky:
    Jimmy and Margaret Banks

From Edinburg, Scotland:
    George Cowan

Index

Jayna Oakley

Born and raised in Lexington, Kentucky with two brothers, Jayna has been around sports all her life. She played on the first girls' high school basketball team at Bryan Station and went on to play softball for the University of Kentucky. She received her bachelor's degree in journalism and began her career as a sports writer before crossing the media line to become a public relations director. She has written for newspapers, magazines, professional journals, as well as created marketing awareness for companies and their employees. Jayna is presently the executive director for the YWCA of Lexington. She likes to play golf, attend sports games to watch her niece and nephews play, work on crafts with her parents and visit with her grandmother.

Kelli Oakley

Kelli René Oakley, a Lexington, Kentucky native, earned her degree in education at Western Kentucky University. She is currently employed by the University of Kentucky in special events, including marketing at the faculty club. Also, during her tenure at U.K., she has been director of U.K. Catering and the Hilary J. Boone Center in which her responsibilities have included professional banquet dinners, as well as preparing tailgate food for sky boxes at Commonwealth Stadium. Her husband, Jayna's brother, is a high school head basketball coach. She spends time traveling to all of his games as well as participating in their sons' activities. Her spare time is filled with reading, outdoor activities, and cooking. Her kitchen is always open to anyone and everyone! Kelli lives with her husband, Eddie, and their two sons, Ryan and Josh.

KENTUCKY TALEGATING: STORIES WITH SAUCE
Second Edition

If you've enjoyed this first edition of Kentucky Talegating: Stories with Sauce, you will definitely want to be part of our next tailgate cookbook.

Email us your all-time favorite TALEgate stories, recipes, photos and be included in the second edition, KENTUCKY TALEGATING: STORIES WITH SAUCE! If you know when and where you will be tailgating, send us an email with your location and we will arrange an interview and photo session with you to include in the second edition. We need your information by the end of the 2004 football season. Check for updates at our website at www.oakleypress.net. Don't miss out and Happy Tailgating!

KENTUCKY TALEGATING
Jayna Oakley or Kelli Oakley
P.O. Box 911031
Lexington, Kentucky 40591-1031
www.oakleypress.net
oakleys@oakleypress.net
859-277-3732 or 859-223-2614

TALEgate Recipe: You may attach a recipe to this form, if needed.
Categories: Please Circle One:
Appetizers   Salads   Soups   Sandwiches   Main Entrees   Sides   Desserts   Beverages

Name of Recipe:_____
Ingredients:_____
_____
_____
_____
_____
_____
_____

Directions:_____
_____
_____
_____
_____
_____
_____

Number of Servings:_____
Submitted by:
Name_____

Address _____

City _____ State _____ Zipcode _____

Phone Number _____EmailAddress_____

Favorite CollegeTeam_____Favorite High School Team_____

please copy this form and mail to the above address

Kentucky TALEgating: Recipes With Sauce
by Jayna Oakley & Kelli Oakley

Oakley Press
P.O. Box 911031
Lexington, Kentucky 40591-1031
www.oakleypress.net

For Orders Call:
859-277-3732 or 859-223-2614

For Orders Fax:
859-223-2614

Email Orders:
oakleys@oakleypress.net

Please send me _____ copies of

Kentucky TALEgating@	$21.95 each
Postage & handling*	$4.00
Kentucky residents add 6% sales tax	$1.32 each

Total enclosed _____

* Postage & handling charges - $4.00 for first book and $.50 for each additional

Make checks or money order to Oakley Press and mail to:

Oakley Press
P.O. Box 911031
Lexington, Kentucky 40591-1031

Ship to:
NAME _____

ADDRESS _____

CITY _____ STATE _____ ZIP _____